Cambridge Elements ≡

Elements in Modern Wars

RELIGIOUS HUMANITARIANISM DURING THE WORLD WARS, 1914–1945

Between Atheism and Messianism

Patrick J. Houlihan
Trinity College Dublin

CAMBRIDGE
UNIVERSITY PRESS

CAMBRIDGE
UNIVERSITY PRESS

Shaftesbury Road, Cambridge CB2 8EA, United Kingdom

One Liberty Plaza, 20th Floor, New York, NY 10006, USA

477 Williamstown Road, Port Melbourne, VIC 3207, Australia

314–321, 3rd Floor, Plot 3, Splendor Forum, Jasola District Centre,
New Delhi – 110025, India

103 Penang Road, #05–06/07, Visioncrest Commercial, Singapore 238467

Cambridge University Press is part of Cambridge University Press & Assessment,
a department of the University of Cambridge.

We share the University's mission to contribute to society through the pursuit of
education, learning and research at the highest international levels of excellence.

www.cambridge.org
Information on this title: www.cambridge.org/9781009472272

DOI: 10.1017/9781009472241

First published 2024

A catalogue record for this publication is available from the British Library.

ISBN 978-1-009-47227-2 Hardback
ISBN 978-1-009-47226-5 Paperback
ISSN 2633-8378 (online)
ISSN 2633-836X (print)

Cambridge University Press & Assessment has no responsibility for the persistence
or accuracy of URLs for external or third-party internet websites referred to in this
publication and does not guarantee that any content on such websites is, or will
remain, accurate or appropriate.

Religious Humanitarianism during the World Wars, 1914–1945

Between Atheism and Messianism

Elements in Modern Wars

DOI: 10.1017/9781009472241
First published online: June 2024

Patrick J. Houlihan
Trinity College Dublin

Author for correspondence: Patrick J. Houlihan, patrick.houlihan@tcd.ie

Abstract: The history of modern war has focused on destruction; however, practices of saving lives and rebuilding societies have received far less scrutiny. The world wars reconfigured geopolitics on a sacred-secular spectrum dominated by the USA and the USSR. In these events, the motivations of humanitarian actors are disputed as either secular or religious, evoking approval or censure. Although modern global humanitarianism emerged during the world wars, it is often studied in a Euro-centric framework that does not engage the conflicts' globality. The effects of humanitarianism during the Second World War look toward the post-1945 era with not enough reflection on the pre-1945 history of humanitarianism. Thus, what is needed is a critical history beyond moralizing, bringing synchronic and diachronic expansion to study questions of continuity and change. A global history of religious humanitarianism during both world wars places faith-based humanitarianism on a spectrum of belief and unbelief.

Keywords: humanitarianism, human rights, world war, religion, relief and development

ISBNs: 9781009472272 (HB), 9781009472265 (PB), 9781009472241 (OC)
ISSNs: 2633-8378 (online), 2633-836X (print)

Contents

Introduction

The First World War began a global revolution in religious humanitarianism that reconfigured the spectrum of sacred and secular in world affairs. The conflict changed the religious landscape of the globe, expanding religious belief and unbelief to include mass politics motivated by atheism and messianism. At the extreme ends of this spectrum, this resulted in the rise of the Soviet Union, increasingly opposed by the United States.[1] If one views this history as the triumph of secularism, a limited Euro-centric vision misses the vital story of how religiously informed humanitarianism became a major global player in the long-term history of emergency relief to development.[2] This is also a tale of how humanitarianism became intertwined in the global history of human rights.[3] As vital as Europe was, the modern history of religious humanitarianism needs to decenter Europe to account for the extremes of the spectrum: The rise of the USA and the USSR as global superpowers. The emergence of modern China in the twentieth century, from a colonialist object of humanitarian aid transforming into a superpower hegemon and a humanitarian donor, highlights the revolutionary transformations that continue.

What was religious humanitarianism? The deceptively simple starting point is that it was a form of humanitarianism in which faith and beliefs about the sacred mattered, where metaphysics went along with material aid to human beings. However, as Michael Barnett and Janice Stein have written, the attempt to distinguish "faith-based organizations" from "other kinds," including secular ones, is not so easy as it might appear, with scholars making classifications in theory that are much less clear in practice.[4] There are the complications of history with its demands for empirical evidence, context, and viewpoint. At first glance, assessing religious or secular belief looks easy enough for contemporary organizations, many of which talk about themselves in such language and especially in their mission statements. This, however, does not account for history: Organizations are evolving, complex entities with missions that have changed over time. Even regarding entities in the present, there are varieties of individual workers' and donors' motivations, as well as the beliefs and understandings of aid

---

[1] Philip Jenkins, *The Great and Holy War: How World War I Became a Religious Crusade* (HarperOne, 2014).

[2] For the global importance of faith-based humanitarianism in modern history, see Michael Barnett and Janice Gross Stein, eds., *Sacred Aid: Faith and Humanitarianism* (Oxford University Press, 2012).

[3] Michael Barnett, ed., *Humanitarianism and Human Rights: A World of Differences?* (Cambridge University Press, 2020).

[4] Michael Barnett and Janice Gross Stein, "Introduction: The Secularization and Sanctification of Humanitarianism," in Michael Barnett and Janice Gross Stein, eds., *Sacred Aid: Faith and Humanitarianism* (Oxford University Press, 2012), 35–36.

recipients.[5] Contemporary totalizing visions of either sacred or secular at one fixed moment obscure the historical nuances and difficulties of the role of religion in humanitarianism. This phenomenon must be considered on a global spectrum of belief and unbelief with effects that do not offer simplistic, linear, and teleological narratives. Sacred and secular mattered in history, and it is important to keep them in mind about the limits of the analytical spectrum. Nevertheless, instead of polarizing dichotomies that reflect total war's legacies, historical truths about metaphysics and materialism are better studied in an analytical middle ground that does not produce easy, one-sided answers. It is necessary to discuss explicitly faith-based organizations as well as global humanitarian organizations that include some element of religion in their operations along the spectrum of belief and unbelief. There is a wide, sometimes bewildering, variety of humanitarians with different agendas, and this diversity reflects global historical experience.

From worldviews shaped by forms of belief, social action was key to the practice of humanitarianism in the modern world. The etymology of the word "humanitarianism" itself was steeped in religious meaning, and questions of long-term and short-term focus are key to evaluating historical change. "Humanitarianism" was an eighteenth-century theological concept reflecting the "doctrine that Christ's nature was human only and not divine."[6] This theological notion became reframed in the nineteenth century, as humanitarianism began to concern itself with the Social Question inspired by ideas of charity and compassion toward others disadvantaged by new processes of industrial capitalism. The word "charity" had a religious etymology: *Caritas* was a form of love according to the Roman roots that influenced Christian notions of charity. The nineteenth century was a decisive era for the "birth of the modern world" in which humanitarian ideas of charity and compassion started locally and became globalized as never before. As key global histories have shown, the nineteenth century was an age of both secularization and renewed assertion of the sacred, intertwined processes often in tension with each other, helping to transform the world.[7] This interplay of sacred and secular did not stop in 1914; it continued through the upheavals of the twentieth century.

This conceptual history also hints at humanitarianism's relation, but not equivalence, to human rights as an idea of what constitutes the human being.

---

[5] For an excellent overview of attempts to distinguish faith-based and secular organizations, see Gerard Clarke and Michael Jennings, eds., *Development, Civil Society, and Faith-Based Organizations: Bridging the Sacred and the Secular* (Palgrave, 2008).

[6] See "Humanitarianism," *Oxford English Dictionary Online*, www.oed.com/ last accessed December 8, 2023.

[7] C. A. Bayly, *The Birth of the Modern World, 1780–1914* (Wiley-Blackwell, 2004); C. A. Bayly, *Remaking the Modern World 1900–2015: Global Connections and Comparisons* (Wiley-Blackwell, 2018); Jürgen Osterhammel, *The Transformation of the World: A Global History of the Nineteenth Century*, trans. Patrick Camiller (Princeton University Press, 2014).

While human rights thinking was oriented more toward long-term legal frame-works, humanitarianism focused on more short-term existential relief. As humanitarian interventions provided emergency relief, they tended toward main-taining a long-term presence on the ground, in the context of "development." Thus, humanitarianism could change, and sometimes transform, societies for which stabilization was originally the aim. Questions of restorative justice and cultural survival blur the focus between short-term and long-term aims.

The First World War was the world's first "total war," with an unprecedented global shift in the formation of modern beliefs and practices related to views of humanity. Individual and collective identities were rethought: The ways that states used their peoples – and how peoples used their states, as well as an emerging host of nongovernmental organizations that gained global prominence. In the wake of war, masses of people now lacked a clear relationship to either the old or new order in formation. When the old empires and state structures changed or collapsed, new methods emerged to deal with the unprecedented global magnitude of existential suffering. From the ruins of the old regimes, some people no longer fit into the new post-1919 world order, especially refugees and those displaced by war that had shattered imperial systems of governance in 1914. Total war expanded states' war-making capacities, with the resources to wage war increasingly regardless of civilian status. Thus, the First World War caused extreme contradictory actions toward human beings in wartime, with both soldiers and civilians as makers and targets of total war. Depending on viewpoint, the "Other" now could be either an enemy to be destroyed or a fellow human being deserving protection from violence, hunger, disease, and displacement. Beginning in the First World War and taken to a horrific extreme in the Second World War, this destruction and protection would even create a new word, genocide, to describe the targeted extermination of entire categories of people.

The history of the world wars tends to focus on the violence of combat and its life-destroying effects through new industrial technologies designed for mass killing. By contrast, the humanitarian impulse, reaching out to save lives, has received much less comparative historical attention. It is a burgeoning field of inquiry, with modern historians focused on the changes wrought by the First World War. With the beginning of the Italo-Turkish War and the subsequent conflicts of imperial entanglements and population displacements that led to Sarajevo in 1914, the "Greater War" from 1911–1923 is fundamental to understanding modern humanitarianism and war.[8]

---

[8] See Peter Gatrell, Rebecca Gill, Branden Little, and Elisabeth Piller, "Discussion: Humanitarianism," in *1914–1918-Online. International Encyclopedia of the First World War*, eds. Ute Daniel, Peter Gatrell, Oliver Janz, et al., issued by Freie Universität Berlin, Berlin 2017-11-09. https://doi.org/ 10.15463/ie1418.11168; www.1914-1918-online.net. For a monographic interpretation, see

The religious dynamics of this are an inescapable part of understanding humanitarianism and war. Indeed, for the First World War, Branden Little has proposed viewing humanitarianism as the "dynamic of redemptive interventionism" or the "dynamic of salvation."[9] Excellent global histories of humanitarianism place the era of the world wars in long-term perspective, stressing religiosity and religious-inspired thinking as key parts of the analysis.[10] There is a growing historiography on the emergence of humanitarianism in modern times, increasingly with reflection on humanitarianism and human rights.[11]

With limited exceptions, the religious elements of faith-based humanitarianism have been marginalized in secular stories of modernization.[12] Empirically and theoretically, this marginalization misrepresents the key role played by religious humanitarianism during the era of the world wars and the post-1945 era, either through faith-based organizations or with religious ideology as a component. Here, the role of American ideals and practices was inescapable, with religious or quasi-religious ideology a crucial part of worldview projection.[13] In a global competition with the Soviet Union, the USA emerged

---

Bruno Cabanes, *The Great War and the Origins of Humanitarianism, 1918–1924* (Cambridge University Press, 2014).

[9] Branden Little, "An Explosion of New Endeavours: Global Humanitarian Responses to Industrialized Warfare in the First World War Era," *First World War Studies* 5 (2014): 1–16; here, 13.

[10] Two excellent long-term surveys are Michael Barnett, *Empire of Humanity: A History of Humanitarianism* (Cornell University Press, 2011); Silvia Salvatici, *A History of Humanitarianism, 1789-Present: In the Name of Others*, trans. Philip Sanders (Manchester University Press, 2015).

[11] See, for example, John Borton and Eleanor Davey, "History and Practitioners: The Use of History by Humanitarians and Potential Benefits of History to the Humanitarian Sector," in Pedro Ramos Pinto and Bertrand Taithe, eds., *The Impact of History? Histories at the Beginning of the 21st Century* (Routledge, 2015), 153–168; Enrico Dal Lago and Kevin O'Sullivan, "Introduction: Towards a New History of Humanitarianism." *Moving the Social: Journal of Social History and the History of Social Movements* 57 (2017): 5–20; Kevin O'Sullivan, Matthew Hilton, and Juliano Fiori, "Humanitarianisms in Context: Histories of Non-state Actors, from the Local to the Global," Special Issue, *European Review of History: Revue européenne d'histoire* 23, no. 1–2 (2016): 1–15; Johannes Paulmann, "Conjunctures in the History of International Humanitarian Aid during the Twentieth Century," *Humanity: An International Journal of Human Rights, Humanitarianism, and Development* 4, no. 2 (2013): 215–238; Devin O. Pendas, "Toward a New Politics? On the Recent Historiography of Human Rights," *Contemporary European History* 21, no. 1 (2012): 95–111; Bertrand Taithe, "The 'Making' of the Origins of Humanitarianism," *Contemporanea* 18, no. 3 (2015): 485–492.

[12] Focusing on faith-based organizations, some recent works Jamie Furniss and Daniel Meier, "La laïc et le religieux dans l'action humanitaire," *A Contrario: Revue Interdisciplinaire de Sciences Sociales* 18 (2012): 7–36; and Elizabeth Ferris, "Faith-based and Secular Humanitarian Organizations," *International Review of the Red Cross* 87, no. 858 (2005): 311–325. Contemporary perspectives on secularization can be seen in Craig Calhoun, Mark Juergensmeyer, and Jonathan van Antwerpen, eds., *Rethinking Secularism* (Oxford University Press, 2011).

[13] David P. King, *God's Internationalists: World Vision and the Age of Evangelical Humanitarianism* (University of Pennsylvania Press, 2015); Rachel M. McCleary, *Global*

as an economic and cultural superpower during the First World War, with legacies for the contemporary world. It is necessary to rethink the religious elements of humanitarianism and cultural development for the continuities and changes in both world wars.

This Element proposes that including a religious impulse, and particularly the role of faith-based groups and organizations with a religious feature, is a key ideological development that contributes to a global history of humanitarianism from 1914–1945. One needs to look at belief and unbelief in a complicated relationship. By looking at both world wars, one can better appreciate historical continuity and change in the era of total war, looking at the similarities and differences in humanitarian endeavors. This connects the pre-1914 world of European global hegemony with the post-1945 world of European loss of power in the superpower contest of the Cold War dominated by the USA and the USSR – and now, increasingly, China. Vital to understanding processes of humanitarian development, this will involve bringing decolonization movements and the Global South into discussions that are too often Eurocentric. Humanitarianism needs to account for both sacred and secular impulses, which were interrelated and in contestation, especially in the twentieth-century global power struggle that emerged after 1917. Simply reducing everything to religion, or the absence of religion, obscures the motivations of the historical actors on a complex field of mentalities in flux. Nevertheless, there is not a perfect historiographic balance, and this Element will focus on the "faith-based" humanitarian impulses because one needs a counterbalance to the secularizing master narrative.[14]

Humanitarianism was part of the entangled, interreligious history of conflict and cooperation. One must foreground the First World War's legacies and its connections to genocide and human rights development in the Second World War and its aftermath. This includes several key areas of identity formation and nongovernmental organization, assessing the actions and motivations of historical actors (including the agency of victims, resisters, bystanders, and perpetrators), and the vexed questions of justice and remediation. The First World War was the moment when international aid began to focus on civilians, providing immediate relief. The era of the world wars saw the rapid rise of a web of private and public associations often with religiously based missions and goals, also working with an emerging order of international governance and transnational

---

Compassion: Private Voluntary Organizations and U.S. Foreign Policy since 1939 (Oxford University Press, 2009).

[14] For a nuanced philosophical and historical approach that examines religion as the "default option" in premodern society changing to a place as "one option among many," see Charles Taylor, *A Secular Age* (The Belknap Press, 2007).

aid to populations that did not fit the new post-1919 reordering. By contrast, international, intergovernmental planning for the postwar order began before hostilities of the Second World War ceased. Thus, the story of humanitarianism in wartime, while rooted in events of 1914–1945, also challenges these chronological boundaries as insufficient to understanding the historical change of war.

After elaborating on some fundamental actors, actions, and authorial viewpoint in the history of humanitarianism, this Element will proceed in an overall chronological and thematic development. Ambiguities, omissions, and disputations will remain. Certain thematic elements are placed in arbitrary positions in the narrative: for instance, the discussion of the Save the Children Fund, the flu pandemic of 1918–1920, or the role of visual imagery of women and children. These phenomena could be discussed in other sections; nevertheless, their placement in certain sections should provoke reassessments of ideas such as the end of the First World War. Other narrative choices, however, are more deliberate and insistent: for instance, the Nanjing Massacre of 1937–1938 as an event of the global Second World War that challenges the standard Eurocentric periodization of 1939–1945. The Element will conclude with the era of post-1945 humanitarianism and its relevance for the contemporary world.

Who Were the Humanitarian Actors, and How Did They Act?

The humanitarian impulse takes place between diverse groups of historical actors, exacerbated by emergency conditions, especially in times of war. As Didier Fassin has argued, at the heart of humanitarianism is a paradox of unequal power between human beings trying to help other human beings, a "tension between inequality and solidarity." As Fassin elaborates, moral sentiments focus on the "poorest, most unfortunate, most vulnerable individuals" in which the "politics of compassion is a politics of inequality." At the same time, however, the basis of moral sentiments is a "recognition of others as fellows" and thus the "politics of compassion is a politics of solidarity."[15] Continuing the darker implications of this paradox, as Alex de Waal has noted, humanitarian intervention involves fundamental and intrinsic elements of cruelty. Arising from the tension of trying to advance common humanity in the strained circumstances of war, the cruelty can be individual: A clash of ideals and realities, where would-be do-gooders have their ideals dashed by circumstantial constraints and end up feeling themselves to be marginalized failures, having not altered the greater social good. Also, in managing overwhelming needs in desperate circumstances, humanitarians are sometimes

---

[15] Didier Fassin, *Humanitarian Reason: A Moral History of the Present Times*, trans. Rachel Gomme (University of California Press, 2012), 3.

forced to compromise their principles similar to ideas of medical triage. Finally, humanitarians themselves can be blamed for creating impossible dreams for victims, obscuring the fact that an alternate reality is sometimes impossible.[16]

Drawing on the globalization of the American Red Cross, what Julia F. Irwin has called the "humanitarian relationship" took place between donors, would-be donors, authorities (local, national, and international), and recipients of aid.[17] There was a fundamental power dynamic of inequality: The recipients were dependent on foreign aid. The recipients of aid were the most difficult to find an authentic historical voice for, and they must be incorporated into the history of humanitarianism. Beyond wounded soldiers, the most common recipients of aid were now children, widows, and refugees. This was a reversal of the pre-1914 notions of humanitarianism in war, which had focused on soldiers, with international law taking increasing care to specify the distinctions between combatants and noncombatants.

In the hierarchy of needs, humanitarianism was about emergency life-saving relief. The most common aid items were food, clothing, bandages, and medicine. These items combatted the scourges of starvation and disease, providing immediate relief. With lives preserved, concerns for more long-term cultural stability came to the foreground. As time passed, prototypical development work took over as the focus of aid, maintaining and developing schools, missions, and religious institutions as key sites of cultural preservation.

Religious humanitarians professed beliefs that often fell short of their universalist ideals and propagandistic pronouncements. Racism, colonialism, and selectivity toward favored groups highlighted the potential hypocrisy of actions that, despite apolitical intents, were often profoundly political. Charity had limits. The unprecedented destruction of the First World War caused a surge of humanitarian organizations and efforts, increasing in both quality and quantity. Religious humanitarians during the war often stylized their efforts in language of absolute dogmatic conviction and Manichean thinking, in which they, of course, were on the side of light against the darkness. They championed their own cause as moral crusaders creating a new world order and bettering the human condition. This paralleled and reinforced propaganda efforts by the various conflicting states – and sometimes even explicitly using the loaded language of a virtuous crusade. While preaching universalism, religious humanitarians were often unintentionally particular, channeling assistance

---

[16] Alex de Waal, "The Humanitarians' Tragedy: Escapable and Inescapable Cruelties," *Disasters* 34, S2 (2010): S130–S137.

[17] Julia F. Irwin, *Making the World Safe: The American Red Cross and a Nation's Humanitarian Awakening* (Oxford University Press, 2013). See also Little, "An Explosion of New Endeavours," 5–6.

toward members of their own religious faith. It was hypocritical at times, but it was nevertheless historically significant. This was a period of rethinking the human subject and its right to existence. Total war had overturned the stability of prewar society, creating a dynamic new world of uncertainty, despair, and hope for the future. International actors of religious humanitarianism now operated in a transnational framework that went beyond the limits of organized charity in the prewar imperial bourgeois era in which European imperial sovereignty ruled the globe.

Atheism and messianism reconfigured the ideological spectrum, and scholarship of humanitarianism needs to account for the global interaction that the USA and the USSR intervening in world affairs. The Russian Revolution saw the emergence of atheistic communism as a global power player. The pivotal point with the entrance of America into the war was 1917: Wilson's 1916 successful re-election campaign slogan, "He Kept Us Out of War," was quickly discarded in favor of the mantra: "The World Must Be Made Safe for Democracy." The USA and the USSR highlighted the global dimensions of religious humanitarianism in the First World War, yet these powers remain marginalized in the Eurocentric historiography of the conflict, with the American and Russian collective experiences of the First World War as a marginalized war, displaced by the triumphalist collective arcs of twentieth-century narratives.[18] With the fall of the Tsarist Monarchy in 1917, the disappearance of Eastern Orthodoxy and its replacement with a victorious Bolshevistic atheism reshaped the global dynamics of religious interaction. Also in 1917, the evangelistic fervor of the United States, above all its President, Woodrow Wilson, represented the opposite end of the sacred-secular spectrum. Histories of humanitarianism must account for this new globality.

One must explore tensions between sacred and secular in the rapidly changing political context of collapsing empires. This conflict saw the fundamental reordering of ideological power structures, creating the emergence of the modern religious landscape. In Jenkins's portrayal, a geologic metaphor of "tectonic faith" helps to conceptualize how deep traditions suddenly shifted during a period of cataclysmic upheaval.[19] The 1917 collapse of Eastern Orthodoxy's throne-and-altar alliance, coupled with renewed global surges for Judaism, Protestantism, Catholicism, and Islam, helped reconfigure the religious landscape globally. The "normative" model of European secularization, even narrowly conceived in its original theoretical terms, did not fit global

---

[18] Jay Winter and Antoine Prost, *The Great War in History and Historiography* (Cambridge University Press, 2011).

[19] Jenkins, *The Great and Holy War*, 374–377.

events. Thus, whatever secularization took place across post-1945 Europe, one must not consider this a normative global development. Transnational processes like famine and pandemics speak to the contemporary understandings of religiously motivated humanitarianism that approached global dimensions. The legacies of total war continued long after 1945.

Limits of Method

It is necessary to consider a diverse spectrum of religious subjectivities that no one historian can represent. The First World War was the global conflict that reshaped the religious landscape, so one must talk about the interreligious aspects of humanitarianism, even if imperfectly and at times superficially. Representing the current historiography and the author's limits, this Element will restrict itself to the Abrahamic faiths: Judaism, Christianity, and Islam. In the future, non-Abrahamic faiths such as Hinduism and Buddhism should receive justly due attention for their religiosity during the era of the world wars and their role in faith-based humanitarianism. Even given these restrictions, it is apparent that religion during the World Wars involved Jews, Christians, and Muslims in dynamic interaction with each other as well as with diverse groups in their own faith-based communities. This analytical desire for interreligious globality is often constrained by modern historical methods.

Historical research methods of the single researcher militate against telling a global narrative of religious humanitarianism. The historical method often stresses nuance and detail, grounded in thick description of context and archival evidence. This approach for religious humanitarianism often limits analysis to one group, often a singular faith community or nongovernmental organization within the personal interest and language ability of the historian. While methodologically sound for local or regional studies, or for studies of one organization or faith community, this has often hampered more global efforts to tell a "grand narrative" of religious change that involves multiple religions, regions, and rational actors.

This limit is also an advantage, or it can be, if it generates a humility that is a necessary component of a history presuming to tell a religious humanitarian narrative of global relevance. In contrast to scientific certitude and dogmatic declarations, ambiguity and ambivalence are key watchwords of ecumenical, inclusive, contemporary religious pluralism – and thus an anachronism during the conflict itself, which tended toward ideological certainty as well as partiality toward favored groups.

On a fundamental level, no one historian can tell the grand narrative of humanitarianism that binds the global with the local, simply because of the limits of the human person. The lone historian with limited resources, especially language abilities and empirical historical materials to represent the subjective experiences of historical actors. How does one presume to tell a global and local story of religious humanitarianism that can access the organizational records of a bewildering variety of nongovernmental organizations (NGOs)? Furthermore, adding a more bottom-up perspective of cultural history, how can one work of global impact claim to represent the subjective worldviews of historical actors and ultimate recipients of religious humanitarian aid, many of whom were illiterate peasants in such places as Russia, Africa, China, and the Middle East?

The present work, based on the author's own perspective and historical limits, will fall far short of communicating these everyday experiences of vast swaths of the global population. From the author's limited perspectives and university experience, it could be argued that this Element is primarily global along a trans-Atlantic axis, with aspirations toward more comprehensive world-wide coverage. However, this Element will nonetheless outline ways of reconceptualizing the global ideological dimensions of humanitarianism during the world wars.

In this Element, the role of the Catholic Church has received disproportionate attention, of which the author is fully aware and accepts responsibility for shortcomings of coverage as well as errors of fact and interpretation. Non-Catholic religious groups and nonreligious groups both make up essential parts of the history of belief and unbelief, and hopefully, future scholars will develop these aspects in greater detail. The present focus on Catholicism represents the author's historical training and research interests, and this is chosen to provide theoretical and empirical reliability about the book's arguments on a global level. Beyond the author's personal academic background, however, the Catholic Church represents a transnational organization with global ambition and empirical archival records that permit a global historical analysis about continuity and change through the wars, revolutions, and upheavals of the twentieth century.[20] There was no other single organization so similarly situated with relevance to issues of humanitarianism and the spectrum of belief and unbelief. Thus, on a global scale, the Catholic Church's modern history is an opportunity to study the Eurocentrism that existed in 1914 as well as its displacement as one moves closer in time to the contemporary era.

At times, generalizations about continental coverage and demographic trends will have to take the place of individual subjectivity about what individual relief recipients thought about the world-shaping times in which they lived – and how

---

[20] John T. McGreevy, *Catholicism: A Global History from the French Revolution to Pope Francis* (WW Norton, 2022).

their own religious subjectivities framed their interpretations of events, particularly the idea of religiously based aid. Nevertheless, by telling a global story, however superficial and inadequate, this work is comfortable with providing some pathways upon which future generations can follow. Acknowledgment of fallibility and shortcomings is appropriate for believers, nonbelievers, and practicing historians. This author is satisfied with not being the final word on the subject, which is a delusive presumption for a dynamic historical process of representation and revision that is continuously evolving. If the present work can stimulate future generations of historians to test its arguments, elaborate its details, or revise and contradict its analysis on any level, the present work will have served its purpose in connecting a chain of past, present, and future events. Situating religious humanitarianism during the epochal events of the world wars is crucial to understanding the nuanced sacred-secular subjectivities of the contemporary world. Interpreting historical actors' rationales on the spectrum of secular to religious is a tricky question, but the problem of historical subjectivity is useful for historical questions of belief and practice: and how these served as motivation and action.

The ambivalent nature of humanitarianism poses a challenge for historians writing between cynicism and romanticism in the humanitarian dilemmas of intervention. Selectivity and agency are key historical questions that can help to study who decides and under what conditions humanitarian intervention provides life-saving relief on the principles of independence of action, neutrality, and need-based impartiality. As Michael Barnett has written about humanitarianism's "lived ethics," scholars need to treat religion seriously as the contingent interaction of ideology and practice: as a fundamental source of worldview creation: What people believe and why they act (or at least say they do). Religion is not simply an opiate of the masses that maintains inequality.[21] It is a force to be reckoned with, beyond personal approval or disapproval, as a historically significant part of understanding the modern world.

The First World War: A Human-Caused Disaster

One needs to examine continuity and change through the First World War as a global moment of imperial reordering. There was a "Greater War" beyond the Western Front trenches of 1914–1918, and these geographic realms were important for globally interconnected population politics that began before 1914 and continued after 1918. It is no coincidence that humanitarianism and genocide happened in areas where imperial state structures were shattered most thoroughly by war and political reordering. It makes more sense to speak of

---

[21] Barnett, *Empire of Humanity*, 6–7.

a Greater War that lasted from 1911–1923 with pre-1914 imperial disruptions that caused land resettlement and population migrations beginning with the Italo-Turkish War of 1911–1912, leading into the Balkan Wars and the 1914 July Crisis that became global and lasted through the violence of the Russian Civil War.[22]

The First World War was a profound moment in the history of humanitarianism because total war had changed the compact between states and citizens. In the imperial state structures of the old order, hierarchically ordered class societies did not organize aid on a mass scale. Reflecting Christian norms of bourgeois morality, trans-Atlantic organizations were dedicated to isolated issues such as the abolition of slavery and the prohibition of trafficking in women. This philanthropy was based on local initiatives and the charity of wealthy individuals. As the scale of warfare expanded, the nineteenth century saw efforts to organize collective institutions, most famously the Red Cross, to alleviate the misery of warfare. Total war, however, brought total claims of states on the human resources of their populations. States mobilized resources but also fell short of meeting citizens' basic needs, especially in areas occupied by imperial powers that lost the war: Germany, Austria-Hungary, Russia, and the Ottoman Empire. The politics of food and health became one of the war's most obvious measures for assessing who won and who lost the war. As old empires collapsed, their legitimacy faded as paternalistic emperors could not feed their starving citizen subjects. Nongovernmental organizations stepped in to fill the void as never before: There was no alternative to meet the scale of the mass suffering. The contemporaneous collapse of the Romanov, Hohenzollern, Habsburg, and Ottoman empires created a humanitarian crisis unprecedented in history.

Moral principles had been enshrined in humanitarian law in the decades before the First World War, trying to limit the destructiveness of combat. The Battle of Solferino (June 24, 1859) was an epic moment in the emergence of the Red Cross. Much of humanitarian law in the Hague Conventions centered on identifying soldiers and civilians, identifying rights and responsibilities to spheres of conflict that created a demarcated zone of battle apart from the "normative" peacetime realm of civilians. The First World War would help to erase these boundaries between soldiers and civilians as entire nations became components of their states' war-making ability. Consequently, the war touched the lives of populations as never before, overwhelming extant humanitarianism. From this crisis there also arose opportunity, creating a new wave of NGOs.

---

[22] Robert Gerwarth and Erez Manela, eds., *Empires at War, 1911–1923* (Oxford University Press, 2014).

The totalizing war saw industrial carnage wreaking havoc on soldiers and civilians on an unprecedented global scale. Prisoners of war, disabled soldiers, war widows, and orphans became prominent groups in humanitarian thinking, now much more visible to civilian populations. The war also increased the massive destabilization of populations. Refugees and migrants became visible actors culminating in the new symbolism of women and children as helpless victims of war. Hunger politics was a weapon of economic and commercial total war, with empires trying to starve each other's populations into submission. Massive famines caused millions' starvation deaths and made populations more vulnerable to diseases. War, civil war, revolution, and counterrevolution caused massive suffering on a global scale.

For the International Committee of the Red Cross (ICRC), the First World War was a profound shift in the aims and means of the Geneva Committee and its various national societies, changing the organization's aims and deeds. Awarded the Nobel Peace Prize in 1917, the ICRC took a new "active role as a neutral intermediary between the warring countries" focusing on two key aims: (1) assessing violations of the Geneva Convention and (2) protecting prisoners of war. The ICRC's efforts were based on the precedents of the Balkan Wars, with legislative reference to the 1907 Hague Conventions. Now that totalizing war had broken out across the globe, however, the field for humanitarian action had increased. The ICRC organized huge efforts to trace soldiers, contact families, facilitating exchanges of information as well as letters and packages. It initially made its reports on war conditions to the public, and later to countries involved.[23] "Impartiality" and "neutrality" became key concepts, crucial toward interpreting humanitarian organizations' legitimacy. The diplomatic framework during wartime was a vicious struggle between the Great Powers, and a new nongovernmental international framework was emerging because of the battlefield impasse.

The origins of modern humanitarian organizations serving wartime needs were focused on wounded soldiers. Jean Henri Dunant was inspired to develop the Red Cross after witnessing the Battle of Solferino (1859). Gendered in religious tropes of the Virgin Mary, women became prominent leaders who tapped into the religious piety of the nineteenth century, including battlefield suffering. Prominent women included Florence Nightingale during the Crimean War (1853–1856) and Clara Barton, the "Angel of the Battlefield," during the United States Civil War (1861–1865). In the US Civil War, early pioneering photographers like Matthew Brady and Alexander Gardiner made photo representations of the stark horrors of war showing mangled bodies on battlefields

---

[23] Salvatici, *A History of Humanitarianism*, 72.

such as Antietam (Sharpsburg) and Gettysburg. During the First World War, the symbolic visual imagery and representation changed to focus on starving emaciated women and children, as the ultimate victims of war, highlighting the costs of total war.[24]

Prisoners of war became a major focus of humanitarian intervention.[25] POW camps were sites of religious exchange because soldiers had a right to religion that was increasingly recognized in international law. Article 18 of Hague IV (1907) declared that "Prisoners of war shall enjoy complete liberty in the exercise of their religion, including attendance at the services of whatever church they may belong to, on the sole condition that they comply with the measures of order and police issued by the military authorities."[26] Religious networks helped maintain bonds of solidarity between homefront and battlefront, with states and NGOs organizing provisions to ensure that POWs had opportunities to practice their religion. This record-keeping bureaucracy was involved in tracking soldiers' identities. Military chaplaincies of the belligerents sent religious officials who served in the POW camps and tried to provide adequate pastoral care for POW soldiers. Chaplains were focal points of correspondence between homefront and battlefront, funneling information in both directions.[27]

Similarly, the logic of tracing soldiers' locations led to the involvement of religious organizations in offering last rites and burial of corpses, as well as families' efforts to repatriate the bodies. Religious organizations attempted to provide dead soldiers with a burial according to their religion's rites. In the era before the League of Nations was an international diplomatic forum, religious organizations were a key communication channel between belligerents. Religious organizations steeped in traditional modes of transnational solidarity did not champion individual states during the conflict. The First World War reshaped international humanitarianism, but during the war, most work was done at the national level. Except for Northern France and Belgium, it was impossible for foreign humanitarian organizations to contact civilians in areas like Central and Eastern Europe as well as the Middle East.

During the First World War, however, humanitarianism developed a new focus on civilians. As Tammy Proctor has argued, the category of civilian

---

[24] Michelle Tusan, "Genocide, Famine and Refugees on Film: Humanitarianism and the First World War," *Past & Present* 237, no. 1 (November 2017): 197–235.

[25] Heather Jones, "International or Transnational? Humanitarian Action during the First World War," *European Review of History: Revue européenne d'histoire* 16, no. 5 (2009): 697–713.

[26] For the Hague convention, see https://ihl-databases.icrc.org/applic/ihl/ihl.nsf/0/1d1726425f6955aec125641e0038bfd6 (last accessed December 1, 2023).

[27] Patrick J. Houlihan, *Catholicism and the Great War: Religion and Everyday Life in Germany and Austria-Hungary, 1914–1922* (Cambridge University Press, 2015).

became synonymous with "women and children."[28] Eglantyne Jebb, one of the founders of the Save the Children Fund was arrested in Trafalgar Square in May 1919 because she was distributing leaflets showing pictures of starving German children.[29] During the end phase of negotiations of the 1919 Paris Peace Conference, Britain was still operating a naval blockade trying to compel Germany to sign the Treaty of Versailles. State authority in Britain viewed charity for starving German children as unpatriotic and defeatist. The limits of charity showed the extent to which total war encompassed entire populations, continuing to make war on each other after the guns of the Western Front fell silent. Total war had social and economic aspects integral to how states waged war.

The German invasion and occupation of Belgium and Northern France cast the war in moral overtones. The innocence of Belgium was also gendered with violations of civilian status paramount and in need of special protection and intervention. The Great War added a powerfully enhanced set of visual imagery, with mother and child as refugees from the devastations of war. The "Rape of Belgium" in 1914 provided a sexualized representation of innocence violated by the aggressive Germanic Huns, with the burning library at Louvain a symbol that Germans were barbaric destroyers of Western culture. German atrocities on the Western Front were grounded in the reality of military occupation that violated international law.[30]

The Russian Civil War: Global Atheism and Messianism

For the sacred-secular spectrum of belief and unbelief, it is vital to study the Russian Revolution and Civil War for their relevance to the wave of humanitarianism that occurred in the collapse of empire and the reframing of sovereignty. This entailed vast socio-political restructurings leading to the emergence of the Soviet Union as an atheistic hegemon. The massive suffering caused a rush of humanitarian organizations to fill the roles of social outreach when traditional structures collapsed. The faith-based messianism of the USA and the state-sponsored atheism of the (eventual) USSR were together on a world-historical stage.

The American Relief Administration (ARA) was one of the clearest examples of the new global world order in which religiously inspired humanitarianism had reframed the sacred-secular spectrum. The ARA, directed by Herbert Hoover, had been established to provide food aid to Belgium in 1914

---

[28] Tammy M. Proctor, *Civilians in a World at War, 1914–1918* (New York University Press, 2010).

[29] Emily Baughan, *Saving the Children: Humanitarianism, Internationalism, and Empire* (University of California Press, 2021).

[30] John Horne and Alan Kramer, *German Atrocities 1914: A History of Denial* (Yale University Press, 2001).

under the auspices of the Commission for Relief in Belgium (CRB). Befitting the training of its director, the CRB worked in highly coordinated fashion with almost military-like engineering precision. Belgian refugees captivated the conscience of the Western world, and it was no coincidence that Agatha Christie, who became the world's best-selling English-language novelist, made her most famous fictional detective, Hercule Poirot, a Belgian refugee. The ARA, following the campaign of Aid for Belgium, was one of the primary vehicles for American humanitarian intervention in the new global order. The USA helped to coordinate the joint presence of international, governmental, and private resources through the ARA and the Near East Relief campaign for refugees.[31]

Herbert Hoover was a Stanford-trained engineer who would become a key agent in global arguments about social policy intervention, demonstrating the competing merits of capitalism versus communism: both in the Great War and during his tenure as President of the United States of America from 1929–1933. Hoover wrote to William Haskell, director of the ARA's Russian operations, stating that, the "service that we are able to perform must be given in a true spirit of charity. There must be no discrimination as to politics, race, or creed. Charity can take no interest in international politics, and any individual who does not so conceive his work should immediately be withdrawn upon your initiative."[32]

Hoover wanted to use the ARA to promote stability and reconstruction, thus ensuring repayment of war credits and guaranteeing US exports. Stemming Bolshevism was a top priority for Hoover, who was a visceral anti-Communist. American socialists identified Hoover as "the most obstinate anti-Bolshevik [in the Harding administration]" contrasted with Fridtjof Nansen, described in a June 1920 letter to Lenin as "always one of the most outstanding representatives of the leftist intelligentsia which insisted on reconciliation with Soviet Russia."[33] Hoover and Nansen argued with each other about control of food distribution and the social benefits of food assistance in Russia. The ARA had many more resources than Nansen's organizations, and the ARA often won out. The Bolsheviks were also desperate to stabilize their control of Russia during famine and the Civil War, so they allowed Hoover's ARA into Russia despite misgivings.

---

[31] Salvatici, *A History of Humanitarianism*, 81–82. See also George H. Nash, *The Life of Herbert Hoover: The Humanitarian, 1914–1917* (WW Norton, 1988); Elisabeth Piller, "American War Relief, Cultural Mobilization and the Myth of Impartial Humanitarianism, 1914–17," *Journal of the Gilded Age and Progressive Era* 17, no. 4 (October 2018): 619–635.

[32] Hoover Institution Archives, Stanford University, ARA, Russian Operations, 1919–1925, Box 19, Folder 6, quoted in Cabanes, *The Great War and the Origins of Humanitarianism*, 194–195.

[33] Quoted in Cabanes, *The Great War and the Origins of Humanitarianism*, 195.

Hoover's ARA showed that charitable organizations were replacing individual charity, even organized by singular powerful groups of moral advocates like the Quakers/Society of Friends. Although Hoover had been born and raised a Quaker, he was critical of the organization's approach to charity. Instead, his engineering education and social-planning approach won out: Hoover advocated a scientific approach to public relief based on modern philanthropy through institutions for entire societies. It was a propaganda campaign in which the press would shape public opinion, with the "Red Scare" of 1919–1920 providing a mobilizing ideology for US involvement in Europe. Hoover's socio-political interventionism was a structured form of private–public activism that would later be misleadingly characterized as laissez-faire economics due to the political representations of Franklin Roosevelt's campaign in the 1932 US Presidential election.

The American relief workers believed that their efforts had a religiously tinged notion of divine providence aiding the cause in Russia. The scope of the famine problem and the vastness of governing agriculture in Russia lent existential trans-historical dimensions to the cause of aid. When US grain shipments arrived in 1922, it seemed like salvation was at hand. Will Shafroth wrote that, "The United States can have a solemn feeling of pride in saving the Russian race from extinction ... To the [simple Russian peasants] American inspectors were almost gods. I have seen them crowd around and fall on their knees trying to kiss my feet because I symbolized to them the nation that was saving them from death. And I believe that they will always feel unceasing gratitude to the American people."[34] Drawing on a religiously inspired sense of mission, Colonel Haskell wrote to Hoover in August 1923 that "To the mind of the Russian common people, the American Relief Administration was a miracle of God which came to them in their darkest hour under the stars and stripes."[35] These ideas allowed American aid workers to rationalize their beliefs, affirming the goodness of themselves and their mission.

The idealistic Americans of Hoover's ARA met harsh reality in the Russian famine. In May 1922 Frank Golder, a recent 24-year-old Harvard graduate oversaw the famine relief efforts in the Nikolayev province of which 580,000 of the province's 1.4 million people were suffering from hunger.[36] The medical personnel among the relief staff adapted "shell shock" to "famine shock," portraying the effects on relief workers. In the words of William Haskell,

---

[34] Hoover Institution Archives, Stanford University, ARA, Russian Operations, 1919–1925, Box No. 81, Folder No. 8, quoted in Cabanes, *The Great War and the Origins of Humanitarianism*, 238.

[35] Hoover Institution Archives, Stanford University, ARA, Russian Operations, 1919–1925, Box no. 340, Folder No. 3, quoted in Cabanes, *The Great War and the Origins of Humanitarianism*, 238.

[36] Quoted in Cabanes, *The Great War and the Origins of Humanitarianism,* 234.

describing efforts in the Samara province in the Autumn of 1921: "Many clever young Americans had to be sent out of Russia with nerves completely wrecked or on the verge of insanity due not only to the horrible suffering which they were forced to witness but to the interference and annoyance to which they were unnecessarily subjected by the very soviet officials who should have been their helpers."[37]

When the Tsarist monarchy collapsed in 1917, the influence of Orthodoxy on the Eurasian continent began to wane. The atheistic Bolsheviks would triumph in the Russian Civil War (1917–1923), but in the initial stages of the conflict, the uncertain outcome was greeted with enthusiasm by other religious traditions. The downfall of Tsarist Orthodoxy now meant that Eurasia was a mission field, with global possibilities for the advancement of Catholicism and Protestantism in particular. The twentieth-century experience of Russia represented the vast shift in the spectrum of religious influence in public: from sacred to secular and back to sacred, if one considers the official proclamations of President Vladimir Putin's government. The state-sponsored atheism of the Soviet period drove religion underground but did not quell it. Yuri Slezkine has argued that the constructed domesticity of Bolshevism, both literally and figuratively, shows that Bolsheviks were millenarians, though it is contested whether this millenarianism had any relation to a concept of religion.[38] Histories of belief and unbelief must account for the place of atheism. Declaring everything to be religious reduces the analytical scope and thus the effectiveness of the concepts of religion and atheism. If the Bolsheviks, the most militantly self-declared and politically assertive atheists in history, were actors acting quasi-religiously, then by such logic, no one in history was truly without religion. One must question such conclusions. Historians must take account of unbelievers' professed motivations, too, without assuming that declared unbelief is a form of belief. The spectrum of belief and unbelief must include a place for atheism.

Along the spectrum of belief and unbelief, Archbishop Tikhon, the Patriarch of Moscow, was one religious official who witnessed the vast shift of loyalties firsthand. Tikhon had helped Tsar Nicholas II bless the troops departing for battle in 1914. With the abdication of the Tsar, and the uncertain possible return of a Romanov successor, the Russian Orthodox Church was in a tense relationship with the new Provisional Government under Kerensky. Eventually, the

---

[37] Hoover Institution Archives, Stanford University, William Haskell Papers, 1932, vol I, 157, ARA, Russian Operations, 1919–1925, quoted in Cabanes, *The Great War and the Origins of Humanitarianism*, 235.

[38] Yuri Slezkine, *The House of Government: A Saga of the Russian Revolution* (Princeton University Press, 2017). See also Victoria Smolkin, *A Sacred Space Is Never Empty: A History of Soviet Atheism* (Princeton University Press, 2018).

Bolshevik consolidation of power meant that Tikhon had to flee Russia. The Old Believers became an embattled community both in Russia and as diasporic refugees abroad, believing in a restoration of the divine order that had been disrupted in 1917.

The power vacuum of the Russian Civil War tempted foreign intervention, especially by the bourgeois and aristocratic believers in the old order. Herbert Hoover's ARA was one of the most prominent humanitarian organizations attempting to stop the spread of Bolshevism, attempting to win hearts and minds at the soup kitchen. Lenin's competing slogan of "Peace, Land, Bread" was a compelling counteroffer. Across the globe, people looked at Russia with both hope and despair. Everyone recognized, however, that mass social stability was now a precondition for loyalty to the regimes. A fundamental contest of worldviews nonetheless agreed on the importance of ensuring the health and well-being of all citizens.

The Russian peasants' interpretation of such aid was difficult to gauge. It was a rural, traditional, closed society in which most people lived their entire lives within 30 miles of where they were born. Serfs had been theoretically emancipated in 1861, but many labored in extremely harsh conditions that had not dissipated in 1917. Folk wisdom and traditional religious practices remained, with icons of the saints occupying prominent places in the huts of the *muzhik*.[39] It was only Stalin's collectivization plans in the 1930s that modernized Soviet agriculture at a staggering, murderous human cost. During the Civil War, James Rives Childs, the district supervisor for Kazan remarked in his diary that, "Even when the people of Karakulinsky *volost* were told that the food which we were distributing came from America, there were many to whom this meant nothing as they had no conception of American or of anything outside the narrow little circle in which they moved."[40] Interpreting the recipients' feelings would continue to be a problem for historians and practitioners of development aid.

Language formed one of the essential international communications channels. For Americans operating in Russia and the Middle East, this often formed a barrier to understanding what the aid recipients were feeling, sometimes even failing to understand their basic lifesaving needs. Knowledge of Russian, Arabic, Turkish, and other languages was severely limited for many Americans in the era before the First World War. Consequently, relief workers without appropriate communication skills were desperate for interpreters. In some cases, relief workers had to rely on local guides who, especially in the case

---

[39] Orlando Figes, *A People's Tragedy: The Russian Revolution, 1891–1924* (Viking, 1997).

[40] James Rives Childs, *Black Lebeda: The Russian Famine Diary of ARA Kazan District Supervisor J. Rives Childs, 1921–1923*, ed, Jamie H. Cockfield (Mercer, 2006), p. 167, quoted in Cabanes, *The Great War and the Origins of Humanitarianism*, 238.

of Russia, turned out to be sympathetic to the Bolsheviks, sometimes as spies and political informants.[41]

The battle for the hearts and minds of the Russian people saw Lenin and the Bolsheviks try to downplay the influence and malign the motives of the ARA. The Bolsheviks' propaganda campaigns stressed the firmness of the proletarian solidarity that the October Revolution of 1917 had created, not the humanitarian values, which they maligned as "bourgeois." Bolshevik propaganda often stressed the vast resources of the USA, arguing that American aid to Russia was only a charitable pittance in comparison to the vast wealth of fat, urbane, and finance capitalists. The Bolsheviks tried to counter the influence of the ARA by organizing their own efforts with more left-leaning international NGOs and by launching propaganda campaigns against the ARA. Championing more isolated, class-based international organizations (with less overall resources in terms of financing and personnel), Lenin highlighted the efforts of the International Workers' Committee for Aid to the Starving in Russia, which had the support of Henri Barbusse, Käthe Kollwitz, and George Bernard Shaw, among others.[42] Of course, despite Lenin's enmity, the famine was so devastating that the Bolsheviks were forced to rely on the aid of their ideological opponents like the ARA. In this contest for the hearts and minds of millions, "The moral economy that was the very foundation of rural Russian society was shaken."[43] Central government and local authorities were incapable of dealing with the scope of the famine.

Making the Modern Middle East: Reconfiguring the Holy Land

Ottoman imperial sovereignty collapsed in the Middle East during the Great War, causing a vast humanitarian crisis. Famine and disease reigned, and the Ottoman Empire could not stem the disorder. It has been argued that "modern humanitarianism" was first established in the Middle East during the First World War, essentially secular in outlook.[44] How strong was religious identity a factor in the First World War in the Middle East? For many scholars trained in European history, the question seems like an obvious component but is reductionist when it becomes the overriding or even monocausal explanation. For many scholars with more appreciation of the history of the Middle East, however, the opposite impulse is to acknowledge that religion was a key factor in identity formation, though not the only one or even the most important.

---

[41] Little, "An Explosion of New Endeavours," 9.

[42] Cabanes, *The Great War and the Origins of Humanitarianism*, 239.

[43] Cabanes, *The Great War and the Origins of Humanitarianism*, 239.

[44] Keith David Watenpaugh, *Bread from Stones: The Middle East and the Making of Modern Humanitarianism* (University of California Press, 2015).

One must go beyond stereotypes of religious conflict endemic to the region, with religious division supposedly the main causal factor in explaining the history of the modern Middle East. More recent historians have stressed that religion was an inescapable part of the motivations of crucial historical actors involved, a key factor in Orientalist projections of mission and imperialism. This changed the on-the-ground reality of peaceful religious co-existence in this region since the Crusades. As a foreign intervention in the Middle East ended when funds to organizations dried up and organizations left the region, mission-aries remained with their "civilizing" missions. In a path-breaking work of nuanced critical reflection, Davide Rodogno has written that, "historians who wish to foreground the birth of modern humanitarianism must find a way to accommodate within that modernity the missionaries who often spearheaded aid efforts, and, more broadly speaking, to accommodate religion and Christianity particular, as well as Christianity as multifariously perceived and in relation to Islam."[45]

In the Middle East region, the collapsing Ottoman Empire led to religiously inspired humanitarianism in conflict on the sacred-secular spectrum between the forces of nationalism and colonialism. Charity toward the poor had been one of the central pillars of Islam. European powers had conducted humanitarian interventions, under the guise of being "against massacre," but such interven-tions often contained advancement of imperial agendas.[46] As Keith Watenpaugh and others have shown, in the Ottoman Empire of the late nine-teenth century the Islamic holy endowment administration, *waqf*, had passed from control of Muslim clerics into a semi-private philanthropy that was an increasingly bureaucratized enterprise partially under control of the state.[47] The Ottoman Red Crescent society was established after the Treaty of Berlin (1878), as an analog to the Red Cross. It remained dormant until the Balkan Wars reawakened it, and it became a symbol of Ottoman modernity displayed by the Ottoman elite. The Ottoman Empire also maintained subnational units of the branches of the Red Cross, and poignantly, the Armenian Red Cross.[48]

Due to war, the refugee flow began before the guns of August 1914. With the Italo-Turkish War of 1911–1912, Italian territorial ambitions began the process of reconfiguring the Mediterranean region that only would end with the collapse

---

[45] Davide Rodogno, *Night on Earth: A History of International Humanitarianism in the Near East, 1918–1930* (Cambridge University Press, 2021), 24, 313.

[46] Davide Rodogno, *Against Massacre: Humanitarian Interventions in the Ottoman Empire, 1815–1914* (Princeton University Press, 2011).

[47] Watenpaugh, *Bread from Stones*, 8.

[48] The symbolism of Red Crescent and Red Cross, however, implies that religious identity was important as a signifier of identity, regardless of the degree of secularism practiced by the respective organizations. Watenpaugh, *Bread from Stones*, 10.

of fascism in 1945. At the beginning of the twentieth century, this war-making encouraged other states to take territory from the Ottoman Empire, causing the Balkan Wars. The events of the July Crisis of 1914 were in some ways a Third Balkan War that ignited a global war. The Italo-Turkish War saw aerial bombardment as a new form of combat, creating a way of killing enemies at a distance previously unknown. Severely outnumbered, the Ottoman Army used guerrilla tactics. Most infamously in the Tripoli Massacre of 1911, the Italian Army responded with reprisals that included the systematic murder of civilians, including burning 100 refugees who had taken shelter in a mosque.[49]

The Balkan states took advantage of the Ottoman Empire's weakness, declaring war and seizing territory. As the Balkan states fought the Ottomans (and then amongst themselves), the ensuing wars generated refugees that the Ottoman state struggled to resettle. Population displacement in war aggravated a policy of agricultural consolidation that had taken place as the Ottoman state tried to redefine its landowning policies and maximize agricultural outputs' utility. With the threat of invasion looming in April 1915, the Ottoman state became even more paranoid about potential subversive populations disturbing its shaky control of landowning and agricultural outputs. The wartime search for scapegoats would culminate in the genocide of the Armenians.

The plight of the Armenians received international attention. In the 1915 Joint Declaration of France, Great Britain, and Russia, the draft proposal highlighted "crimes against Christianity and civilization," reflecting the influence of Russian Orthodoxy's sense of protectionism during Tsar Nicholas II's reign. This would become "crimes against humanity and civilization." After the objections of France and later Britain, worried about their Muslim subjects in their empires, the Great Powers decided not to restrict the victimhood to Christianity. Furthermore, Armenian groups pressured the Russian government to hold members of the Turkish government responsible "for the love of humanity." Thus, the final Joint Declaration named specific sites of massacres and referred to "new crimes of Turkey against humanity and civilization." The Allied governments were supposed to "hold personally responsible" all those implicated in the massacres. This personal responsibility never happened. The Treaty of Sèvres of 1920 did not enforce the point, and the Treaty of Lausanne of 1923 had a declaration of amnesty.[50]

The Balkan Wars of the early twentieth century caused a retreat of Ottoman power from the region, creating a flow of refugees and migrants. This would create state and local resettlement patterns and conflicts that changed land-

---

[49] Vanda Wilcox, ed., *Italy in the Era of the Great War* (Brill, 2018).

[50] Taner Akçam, *The Young Turks' Crime against Humanity: The Armenian Genocide and Ethnic Cleansing in the Ottoman Empire* (Princeton University Press, 2012).

holding patterns to control nomadic population displacements. Especially in inner Anatolia, state authorities revised settlement patterns that increasingly favored Muslim majorities in rural areas and led to massacres of Armenians in the 1890s and 1909, with new Muslim inhabitants replacing Armenian populations. Thus, according to Watenpaugh, the prewar Ottoman tendencies that became a concerted program of genocide had important prewar roots as a "permanent regime of communal dispossession that accompanied mass killing."[51] Sunni Muslims were the primary administrators and recipients of the Ottoman state's effort, as they were seen to be most useful to the Ottoman imperial state.[52] The efforts to alleviate suffering in one Islamic community caused the suffering of other Christian communities, culminating in genocide. Armenians and non-Muslim subject populations became placed outside the circle of care that the state demonstrated for its increasingly favored Muslim majorities, even in the prewar era. Exacerbating prewar tendencies in the fevered atmosphere of multi-front invasions after Gallipoli in 1915, the Ottoman Empire state made war on itself, using its coercive violence on its own citizen-subjects.[53]

Religion in modern war changed the nature of citizenship. Thus, in identifying notions of citizenship and universalism, religious identity became a key frame of cultural reference for humanitarianism. This was so even when humanitarian relief workers, and their modern bureaucratic apparatuses, styled themselves as increasingly secular. Around 1.5 million Christians were killed by Muslims in the genocides of the Great War. Religious identity became a marker of difference that became increasingly ethno-nationalized. Religious difference in the context of war's extreme measures thus created unstable boundaries, helping to dismantle imperial notions of citizenship in which Muslims, Christians, and Jews in the Holy Land had lived together under the protection of the Ottoman Empire since the medieval era.[54]

There were elements of interreligious cooperation, most notably in urban centers, especially Constantinople. There, the Ottoman Red Crescent Society cooperated with the Rockefeller Foundations War Relief Board to establish soup kitchens and orphanages that served Muslims, Jews, and Christians alike in the war's early phase. This ended by 1916, as the Rockefeller Foundation's representative, Edward R. Stoerer, noted that the Ottoman political elite resented the "outside" help. Stoerer was the Rockefeller Foundation's Istanbul representative who noted that according to the Ottoman elite "it was undignified

---

[51] Watenpaugh, *Bread from Stones*, 11.   [52] Watenpaugh, *Bread from Stones*, 12.

[53] Watenpaugh, *Bread from Stones*, 13.

[54] Ronald Grigor Suny, *"They Can Live in the Desert but Nowhere Else": A History of the Armenian Genocide* (Princeton University Press, 2015).

to receive active help from the outside and an inclination to resent the suggestion that it was necessary. Though at all times money given outright to them to be administered by their own agents would have been acceptable." The Red Crescent society had emerged from the aftermath of the Treaty of Berlin. The Ottoman Red Crescent Society became involved in the transfer of Armenian children. This was one of the genocide's most religiously loaded and politicized aspects: Religious differences became politicized as ethno-national difference was polarized in religious terms.[55]

The Middle East region saw immense reordering during the events of the Great War and its aftermath, leading to complicated histories of empire, humanitarian relief, international mandate supervision, and complicated memory politics of community formation. As Melanie S. Tanielian has shown on the local level for Lebanon and particularly Beirut, the crumbling Ottoman state during wartime was not successful in its own efforts at the city level to organize humanitarian famine relief. American wartime neutrality meant that missionaries and educators were connected to the Ottoman state, yet their efforts "stood outside obligatory communal patronage," leading to relative successes compared to direct Ottoman state involvement, successfully positioning America as "*the* benevolent power" in terms of humanitarian aid. These networks of foreign missionaries and educators coordinated their humanitarian efforts with international organizations including the Red Crescent and Red Cross.[56] The development of the Red Crescent in the modern Middle East highlights comparative regional histories in the era of the World Wars: with vast devastation and reordering for both Europe and the Middle East during the First World War; however, the Middle East region did not undergo a comparable experience of the Second World War, largely escaping the destruction of total war that shattered Europe. The increased presence of Islamic faith-based organizations became a part of this landscape in the post-1945 period, complicating simplistic notions of secular or sacred teleology.[57]

Orientalist conceptions of Ottoman backwardness convinced Western powers that the Ottoman empire was barbaric and beyond reform if left to itself. Regardless of the secularizing development of the late Ottoman Empire, there was a strong religious impulse on the part of Western humanitarian relief workers, bent on setting a Christian example in the Holy Land: Which often meant helping exclusively Christians. The Ottoman state took note of this

---

[55] Watenpaugh, *Bread from Stones*, 13, 11.

[56] Melanie S. Tanielian, *The Charity of War: Famine, Humanitarian Aid, and World War I in the Middle East* (Stanford, 2018), 250.

[57] Jon Alterman and Karin von Hippel, eds., *Understanding Islamic Charities* (Center for Strategic & International Studies, 2007).

disregard for non-Christians by Western humanitarians, thus bolstering the Ottoman state's own humanitarian efforts to reach out to Muslim communities, both before and during the Great War. Perceived Western indifference to Muslim suffering became a refrain that led to relativism that could include genocide denial.[58]

In the Holy Land, the collapse of the Ottoman Empire reshaped the socio-religious landscape of the region. Orientalist ideas of supposed Ottoman backwardness shaped how Western powers saw Muslim-ruled empires. This outlook determined humanitarian interventions in the Middle East in many contemporary explanations of the conflict and the postwar settlements and occupations. As Watenpaugh has argued, the secular dimensions of humanitarianism in the Middle East had central elements of pre-1914 policies of displacement and possession related to the Ottoman Empire's migrant resettlements in the aftermath of the Balkan Wars. This displacement of communities spoke to the "cruel logic of organized compassion" in which attempts to alleviate one community's suffering caused suffering for another community. This culminated in genocide, with the Ottoman state making war on its own citizens. The centrality of the genocide of the Armenians and Assyrians placed them outside the "circle of care" inherent to humanitarian thinking.[59]

The Orientalist perceptions of Ottomans contained religious elements that were undeniably present in the motivations of contemporary religiously minded Westerners intervening in the Middle East, in military, political, and humanitarian ways. There were strong Anglo-American overtones of a Crusade for Christ with apocalyptic dimensions. British General Edmund Allenby captured Jerusalem on December 9, 1917, entering on foot to show his respect for the Holy City. Catholic churches in Rome rang out the *Te Deum* in celebration. Consciously humbly imitating the example of Christ's entry into Jerusalem on a donkey before the Passion and Crucifixion, Allenby's stylized Christian humility contrasted with the 1898 visit of Kaiser Wilhelm II, for whom the Ottomans had torn down the Jaffa gate so that the Kaiser's entourage could proceed, with the Kaiser at the lead mounted on a white horse and the Kaiserin in a carriage following. Allenby referred to the decisive victory at the battle of Meggido in September 1918 as the "Field of Armageddon" and when he later received a peerage, he was known as Allenby of Armageddon. Contemporary Muslim observers noted that Allenby's surname had prophetic significance: It was similar to *al-Nabi* "the Prophet" with the suggestive resonance of "God, the Prophet," (*Allah Nabi* [Allenby]).[60]

---

[58] Watenpaugh, *Bread from Stones*, 7, 12.   [59] Watenpaugh, *Bread from Stones*, 10–15.
[60] Jenkins, *The Great and Holy War*, 176–181.

Christians rediscovered the Jewish origins of their faith, with apocalyptic visions of Zionism that reinforced the humanitarian notions of a chosen elite aiding the earthly quest for advancing the heavenly kingdom. Writing in exile in St. Gallen, Switzerland, the Rabbi Abraham Isaac Kook, wrote of the eschatological dimensions of the war in his most famous work, *Orot HaKodesh* (The Lights of Holiness) later revered by Israel's Orthodox and ultra-Orthodox. Kook wrote, "The present world war is possessed of an awesome, deep and great expectation attached to the changes of time, and the visible sign of the End in the settlement of the land of Israel." Kook wrote of the need for "Total dismantling of all the foundations of contemporary civilization, with all of their falsity and deception, with all their poison and venom. The entire civilization that rings false must be effaced from the world and in its stead will arise a kingdom of a holy elite." It was a damning indictment of the Great War: "The spiritual fabric that in its present state could not prevent, despite all its glorious wisdom, wholesale slaughter and such fearful destruction, has proven itself invalid from its inception ... and all its progress is not but false counsel and evil entrapment ... Therefore, the entire contemporary civilization is doomed and on its ruins will be established a world order of truth and God-consciousness."[61]

Grounded in Christian notions of charity, the USA was an emerging dominant force in the global field of humanitarian intervention. The ARA and Near East Relief both highlighted the increasing importance of an interventionist mode of mission-based fervor. Founded in 1915 as the American Committee on Armenian Atrocities, which later became the American Committee for Relief in the Near East (ACRNE), and then Near East Relief (NER), the name under which it achieved global takeoff. It became The Near East Foundation (NEF), the name it operates under. The Near East Relief program was a prime example of American mobilized aid for a specific humanitarian cause with a religious background. The program mobilized private citizens with governmental institutions in which US diplomacy was crucial. The original missionary impulse sprang from the American Board of Commissioners for Foreign Missions, especially the ideas of a former missionary and educator James L. Barton, a former missionary and educator, who teamed with the philanthropist Cleveland H. Dodge and Ambassador Henry Morgenthau. The group appealed to a broad US public to help the suffering, starving Armenian Christian people. Stylized in what amounted to crusading terms, this was portrayed to the American public to oppose the perceived barbarity of Muslim Turks against Western Civilization. This generated over $110 million that fed 300,000

---

[61] Quoted in Jenkins, *The Great and Holy War,* 251–252.

people.[62] What began as an appeal to a humanitarian charity focused solely on aiding hunger became an expanded development program in the region that built schools, instituted vocational training, bolstered manufacturing, and created leisure opportunities.

In 1915, the Middle East was in a humanitarian crisis due to multi-year plagues of locusts and extensive flooding. This caused widespread famine of scriptural proportions. A Palestinian serving in the Ottoman military, Ihsan Turjman, noted in his diary: "Monday, March 29, 1915 . . . Heavy rain fell on Jerusalem today, which we needed badly. Locusts are attacking all over the country. The locust invasion started seven days ago. Today it took the locust cloud two hours to pass over the city. God protect us from the three plagues: war, locusts, and disease, for these are spreading through the country. Pity the poor." The year 1915 was, and is, noted as *am al Jarad* – the Year of the Locust, with conservative estimates of 500,000 extra civilian deaths in Greater Syria. Plagues and famines had happened before, but total war made the situation worse, with the Ottoman state requisitioning food, transport, and property. Moreover, the war in the Middle East made the Ottoman state an enemy of the region's two biggest trading powers, Britain and France, whose commercial and imperial interests had been vital to the region's prosperity in the pre-1914 era, also denying export markets for Ottoman commodities like oils and produce.[63]

Appeals were made, but no help was forthcoming in a war that closed the borders of the Ottoman Empire and strained its basic capacities. Relief was concentrated only in the cities of Jerusalem and Beirut, which received attention as a projection of the Holy Land. This contrasted with noninterventions for the flooding of the Tigris in Baghdad. The relief efforts became, in the words of Watenpaugh, a "coalition of Progressives, Zionists, Protestant missionaries, liberal intellectuals, extraordinarily wealthy men, and Arab and Armenian immigrant groups, who formed political organizations and philanthropic foundations centered in New York City. From that coalition emerged the practices, media strategies, idealism, and ethics – the repertoire – of American modern humanitarianism in what those Americans saw as the 'Near East.' "[64]

The New York to Washington conduit of information helped determine US policy toward the region. Reports trickled in, such as this one, from a Rabbi B. Abramovic of St. Louis, who contacted the US State Department in late October 1914 claiming, "Received today cablegram from Central Committee of the Jewish population of Palestine, that they are starving."[65] Leading Jewish

---

[62] Watenpaugh, *Bread from Stones*, 86.   [63] Quoted in Watenpaugh, *Bread from Stones*, 30–32.
[64] Watenpaugh, *Bread from Stones*, 25–26.   [65] Quoted in Watenpaugh, *Bread from Stones*, 37.

figures such as the Zionist Stephen Samuel Wise and the jurist Louis Brandeis helped organize the American Jewish Relief Committee (AJC).[66]

Missionaries formed the main source of personnel for what became the Near East Relief. Consequently, their actions and outlooks would shape even more secular versions of humanitarian relief. The Religious Missions in the Middle East were an effort to proselytize, converting Muslims and Jews into Protestant Christians. The large-scale failure of these missionary efforts thus began to focus on reaching out to various sects of Christianity stigmatized by missionaries as "primitive" or "Oriental": filled with superstition and eastern mysticism. This supposed backwardness stood in contrast to the "progressive" modern Protestant Christianity, which stressed perceived virtues such as education, literacy, technology, and abstemious actions that avoided excesses of pleasures of the flesh such as food, sex, alcohol, or drugs.[67]

The international community created the Armenians as one of the "most deserving" objects of humanitarian compassion, mobilizing global aid in support of this victimized Christian people. Through the League of Nations' representation, then, the global community's abandonment and betrayal was particularly galling, as international pressure accepted the results of the Greco-Turkish War and did not punish Turkey for its "crimes against humanity."[68]

Interwar Years: Civilizing Missions

The history of humanitarianism during the Great War shows that there were important developments both before 1914 and after 1918. As Elisabeth Piller has noted, many humanitarian organizations were founded after the fighting on the Western Front ended.[69] Furthermore, Jay Winter has argued for conceptualizing a Second Great War in the Middle East from 1918–1923 that only concluded with the Treaty of Lausanne (1923) ending the Greco-Turkish War.[70] Many European intellectuals had cheered for their respective states when war broke out in 1914; however, the devastation had caused some prominent thinkers to rededicate themselves to humanitarian visions that also had real world impact to improve the world.[71]

---

[66] Watenpaugh, *Bread from Stones*, 37.

[67] Watenpaugh, *Bread from Stones*, 17–18. The phrasing suggests connotations of viewing recipients and potential subjects for conversion and also objects of humanitarianism.

[68] Watenpaugh, *Bread from Stones*, 28.   [69] Gatrell, Gill, Little, and Piller "Discussion."

[70] Jay Winter, "The Second Great War," *Revista Universitaria de Historia Militar* 7, no. 14 (2018): 160–179. For long-term perspectives, see Jay Winter, *The Cultural History of War in the Twentieth Century and After* (Cambridge University Press, 2022).

[71] Tomás Irish, *Feeding the Mind: Humanitarianism and the Reconstruction of European Intellectual Life, 1919–1933* (Cambridge University Press, 2023).

Rooted in the Italo-Turkish War and the Balkan Wars, refugees and migrants were parts of processes that began before the Great War, yet these events also were exacerbated and forever changed by the war and its consequences. As Peter Gatrell recently has argued, refugees and migrants were key transnational actors in the story of twentieth-century Europe's transformations.[72] Because of total war, refugees became an international problem that gained increasing global awareness. Dwarfed by the scope of refugees from the simultaneous collapse of multiple empires, existing state institutions were unable to solve the issue of migratory flux. The specially appointed League of Nations High Commissioner for Refugees, Fridtjof Nansen, had received pressure from the ICRC President, Gustave Ador, to address the issue. Nansen would win the 1922 Nobel Peace Prize, and the Nansen Passport was the most famous international symbol of refugee aid, but it did not have universal value. It was originally issued to a set of Russian people based on nationality, and it was based on a defined event: namely, the chaos of the Russian Revolution and Civil War. It was later broadened to other selective groups, and it also left open questions of future destiny, with Nansen in favor of repatriations. Overall, the idea reigned those refugees should relocate to a "real" home country with the same nationality, religion, and language.[73] Of course, the disorders caused by the First World War had created a situation of political flux that made such solutions unlikely for what had been multi-ethnic empires. Population exchanges dominated post-1919 reordering, with retroactive legitimation by the League of Nations. National governments and mandatory powers coordinated the population flux, privileging peoples who had representation in the normative nation-state framework that had emerged after Paris 1919. The League of Nations helped to centralize efforts by coordinating organizations like the ICRC, YMCA, the SCF, ARC, and the Friends. The issue of refugees now had international attention that developed beyond Nansen's death in 1930. To continue his work, the League of Nations founded the Nansen International Office for Refugees, which would win the 1938 Nobel Peace Prize.

International humanitarianism in the interwar years tried to go beyond relief: toward development, often with international globalists in a paternalistic framework implementing their worldviews. Indeed, as Davide Rodogno has shown from 1918 into the 1920s, emergency relief transitioned to proto-development. For the Middle East, a region where the First World War's collapse of empires changed utterly, Rodogno has shown how an array of international

---

[72] Peter Gatrell, *The Making of the Modern Refugee* (Oxford University Press, 2013); Peter Gatrell, *The Unsettling of Europe: How Migration Reshaped a Continent* (Basic Books, 2019).

[73] Salvatici, *A History of Humanitarianism*, 94–100; more generally, see Gatrell, *Making of the Modern Refugee*.

humanitarians projected their own domestic and colonial experiences onto their imaginary projections of the Middle East. This highlighted the extent to which relief efforts in this region were transitioning to an idea of proto-development, and in which the ideals of America loomed increasingly large on the stage of international development and global supremacy. The intent for control often fell short of a reality that was confused, ephemeral, and subject to shifting policies. The international humanitarians, in which Protestant American Christianity played a decisive role, were influenced by self-conceptions of enlightened, progressive benevolence and increasing science-based public policy. They had Orientalist projections, full of prejudice against a supposedly backward Islamic Ottoman empire in need of reform and modernization. In the words of Barclay Acheson, the overseas director of the Near East Relief and one of the leaders of the Near East Foundation, "Mohammaden fanaticism" was an ancient feature that combined with the modern import of "materialism" to create an unstable society. According to Acheson, the American civilizing mission of redemptive education was the solution to this instability.[74]

"Civilizing" missions were taking place in humanitarian relief efforts and international diplomacy, both formally and informally. As Susan Pedersen has demonstrated for the League of Nations, the interwar years created networks of international activists, establishing communication channels and modes of cooperation that were tangible successes of global policymaking.[75] The League of Nations was also a centralizing presence that coordinated disparate associations, representing an "institutionalisation of humanitarianism" of contingent and nonlinear processes that reflected "joint presence, negotiation, [and] collaboration" that characterized this flourishing of activities in the 1920s.[76] Unfairly damned in teleological hindsight for its political failures that led to appeasement and the outbreak of World War II, in social policy, the League of Nations was much more successful.[77] The humanitarian networks fostered by League of Nations were an excellent example in the history of humanitarianism, creating informal associations as well as more formalized bureaucratic structures that would rethink the theory and practice of humanitarianism at the local, national, international, and supranational levels. This would inform the United Nations and the NGO movement in the post-1945 era.[78] The Paris Peace Conference of 1919 had positive legacies, too.

---

[74] Quoted in Rodogno, *Night on Earth*, 315.
[75] Susan Pedersen, *The Guardians: The League of Nations and the Crisis of Empire* (Oxford University Press, 2015).
[76] Salvatici, *A History of Humanitarianism*, 82–88.   [77] Pedersen, *The Guardians*.
[78] Salvatici, *A History of Humanitarianism*, 88.

These associational networks were often religiously tinged. Alliances were not always clear-cut, especially in the early phase of sorting out the global world order after 1918. There were rival claimants for religious leadership of humanitarian movements. Pope Benedict XV and Woodrow Wilson were rivals for the role of religiously motivated public leadership. Wilson, with a strong Presbyterian upbringing and self-righteous convictions, made sure that Benedict XV's August 1917 Peace Note did not find an actionable response from the Entente Powers. For his own famous Fourteen Points of 1918, Wilson incorporated many of the same thematic points from Benedict XV's earlier intervention, with Wilson seeing himself as a quasi-Messianic figure heading to Paris in 1919 on a mission of redemptive salvation for the broken world.[79]

Over the course of the twentieth century, the groundwork of post-1945 European unity had an important prehistory in the "interwar" era, as new networks and associations formed. Jean Monnet was one of the key architects of transnational solidarity that would result in the European Union. On October 10, 1919, Monnet advocated that the League rely on the resources of the World Alliance for Promoting International Friendship through the Churches, circulating pamphlets entitled, "The Roman Catholic Church and the League of Nations" and "The World Alliance and International Reconstruction" published by Dr. George Nasmyth, who was a "representative type of the propagandists with whom the League of Nations should get into touch as soon as possible."[80] Nasmyth was a suspected Bolshevik sympathizer, denied entry into the United Kingdom because of his suspected political sympathies, who proposed to establish an International Catholic Bureau at Fribourg, Switzerland, where eventually the related "*Union Catholique études internationales*" was founded by conservative Catholic aristocrats.[81]

Religious missions were one way that European powers continued their prewar "civilizing" ideas, with Christianity as an important ideological background. Britain, France, and the United States continued to exercise a "muscular Christianity" in service of their disparate empires.[82] The Young Men's Christian Association (YMCA) represented a form of muscular Protestant Christianity especially vibrant in the USA and Britain. It brought material and spiritual comfort, especially by supplementing soldiers' rations and fostering collective Bible readings with combat soldiers and POWs on both sides. It presented an

---

[79] John F. Pollard, *The Papacy in the Age of Totalitarianism, 1914–1958* (Oxford University Press, 2014), 67.

[80] League of Nations Archives (hereafter, LON), R.1006/1219/1476; LON R.1006/1219/1219.

[81] Cormac Shine, "Papal Diplomacy by Proxy? Catholic Internationalism at the League of Nations' International Committee on Intellectual Cooperation, 1922–1939," *Journal of Ecclesiastical History* 69, no.4 (2018): 785–805.

[82] LON, R. 9, Doss. 980, "Religious missions in Mandated Territories."

image of ordered domesticity and calm reassurance about Divine Providence that comforted some soldiers in extreme situations. For other soldiers, however, the YMCA's messages of teetotaling and sexual abstinence generated aversion and ridicule.[83] John R. Mott was a crucial leader for the YMCA and its efforts among ecumenical religious humanitarian movements in the era of the world wars. Key to ecumenical striving, the international missionary movement took off after the Edinburgh Missionary conference of 1910.[84] Mott's proposed reforms spoke to the influence of Christianity among the ecumenical movements of the twentieth century, and he would win the Nobel Peace Prize in 1946.[85]

The former German colonies across the globe became part of the mandates, and religion played a role in imperialistic civilizing attitudes via the continued presence of religious missions. This could result in some unlikely new configurations that highlighted complex global and transnational loyalties. It demonstrated the influence of soft-power religious ideology in behind-the-scenes diplomacy, with the League of Nations as one new international arena.[86] On this issue of religious missions, the Catholic Church represented one of the most effective nascent global transnational networks that could put financial resources across global channels in service of ideology.

This included interventions of soft-power diplomacy behind the scenes at the Paris Peace Conference of 1919, in which missionaries, often key humanitarian agents of civilizing missions, were the chief cause of concern. The Vatican had been officially excluded from Paris in 1919, but this was a blessing in disguise for Vatican interests. It allowed the Vatican to pursue its agenda behind the scenes unofficially, without any responsibility for the disastrous political settlement. Yamamoto Shinjiro (1877–1942) was a Japanese naval attaché at Paris in 1919, sometimes confused with Admiral Yamamoto Isoroku (no relation). Yamamoto Shinjiro was a fervent Catholic believer who served as an indirect diplomatic channel, triangulating between the interests of Japan, the Big Four, and the Catholic Church.

One fundamental issue concerned Catholic missionaries on former German colonies in the Pacific islands and in Africa. Bishop (later Cardinal) Bonaventura Cerretti was the Vatican emissary behind the scenes in Paris, working with Yamamoto Shinjiro to advance Vatican interests for missionaries

---

[83] Salvatici, *A History of Humanitarianism*, 76.

[84] Brian Stanley, *Christianity in the Twentieth Century: A World History* (Princeton University Press, 2018).

[85] John R. Mott, "The Future of International Missionary Cooperation," (Pamphlet) (New York: International Missionary Council, n.d.)

[86] LON, R. 9, Doss. 980, "Religious missions in Mandated Territories."

on the Pacific islands. It was an indirect approach to influencing the Great Powers via Catholic emissaries. Cerretti talked about Yamamoto as a good collaborator who allowed access to the President of the Japanese delegation, using Canadian Monsignor Daugherty (described in Vatican documents as "an exemplary Catholic") to get access to Arthur Balfour, the British Foreign Secretary.[87] For getting to President Wilson through Colonel Edward House, Wilson's most trusted advisor, Cerretti used Admiral William S. Benson in a May 26–27 meeting. Through Yamamoto and Cerretti, the Church managed to secure religious protection for Catholic interests, especially in the former German colonies in Asia and Africa, both during the Paris Peace Conference and its aftermath.[88]

Seen through the Vatican's eyes, the great danger was the looming dominance of Anglo-American Protestantism on a global scale, especially the quasi-messianism of Woodrow Wilson. The Vatican was keenly concerned about Article 122 and Article 438 of the developing Versailles Treaty. Article 438 was altered from the original 6 May version, which as a *NY Times* article opined, "Without alteration, Article 438 would have been the cause of endless disputes."[89] In the 6 May version, religious missions in ex-German colonies would have been managed by commissions of Christians, in which Protestants would have made up the majority and exercised a decisive influence. Allied governments individually could decide to expel German missionaries from colonies. Article 122 remained unchanged, but now Catholic missions would be decided by Catholic commissions. From the Vatican's perspective, this avoided an Anglo-American Protestant land grab, especially restricting Wilson's messianism.

In the former German colonies in the Pacific, Japan expelled German priests, but Yamamoto Shinjiro advocated for Catholic interests with the Japanese government. In an August 10, 1919 letter to Cardinal Pietro Gasparri, the Vatican Secretary of State, Yamamoto wrote of the Japanese intent to preserve good relations with the Catholic Church despite necessary political moves against the Germans. In Yamamoto's words, "Having been forced for political reasons to expel from these islands German Catholic missionaries, but desiring to maintain good relations with the Catholic Church and wanting to maintain the

---

[87] Archivio Storico della Segreteria di Stato – Sezione per i Rapporti con gli Stati e le Organizzazioni Internazionali (hereafter, ASRS), Congregazione degli Affari Ecclesiastici Straordinari (hereafter, AAEESS), AAO III, Pos. 86, Fasc. 60 (Cina 1918–1922. Le Missioni tedesche e la missione di Mons. Cerretti). Fasc. 60, pp. 80–81, Letter, May 31, 1919.

[88] ASRS, AAEESS, AAO III, Pos. 86, Fasc. 60 (Cina 1918–1922. Le Missioni tedesche e la missione di Mons. Cerretti), Fasc. 60, pp. 59–68: note of May 27, 1919.

[89] ASRS, AAEESS, AAO III, Pos. 86, Fasc. 62 (Cina 1918–1922. Le Missioni tedesche e la missione di Mons. Cerretti).

principle of freedom of conscience that the Japanese government has always had," he outlined the measures he was advancing: "(1) That the expelled German Catholic missionaries be replaced by Japanese Catholic priests. (2) That, if too few Japanese Catholic priests cannot fulfill this first wish, the Holy See will send to these islands missionaries already attached to congregations already established in Japan." The latter course of action was adopted.[90]

The transnationalism maintained a Catholic presence in the former German colonies. On October 18, 1919, Pope Benedict XV awarded Yamamoto Shinjiro the Order of St. Gregory the Great (military class), praising the benevolence of the Japanese government on the treatment of missionaries in the Caroline, Marianas, and Marshall Islands, specifically citing Yamamoto's role in fostering diplomacy between Japan and the Holy See. Lay activists such as Yamamoto and his Paris contacts in 1919 highlighted the role of transnational peace networks, operating in a gray zone of official approval between the Great Powers and the hierarchy of the Catholic Church. Much of this lay activism began to flourish in the "Wilsonian moment," with delayed effects in the twentieth century as the Church positioned itself vis-à-vis movements for decolonization and national independence. Yamamoto Shinjiro was a key Catholic channel of religiously influenced diplomacy at Versailles and its global aftermath.

Also due to Catholic involvement, the Save the Children Fund became a global social movement because of a timely religiously motivated intervention in a key early phase of the charity. The Save the Children Fund had origins as a localized British charity, especially through the work of two of its founders, Eglantyne Jebb and Dorothy Buxton, who were sisters. In May 1919, Jebb had been arrested in Trafalgar Square for distributing leaflets that contained pictures of starving German children. With the Treaty of Versailles not yet signed, the hunger politics of British blockade in total war continued, and this humanitarianism for German children was seen as defeatist. Jebb traveled to Rome to enlist the support of Pope Benedict XV who intervened to become the most prominent public support of the SCF in its early phase. The pope had supported children explicitly through initiatives like foundlings' homes in Rome itself and he seized on the opportunity to come out in support of a broad global appeal on behalf of the world's children.[91]

---

[90] ASRS, AAEESS, AAO III, Pos. 110, Fasc. 75, Asia Giappone 1919–1921. Convenzione con il Governo giapponese per la sistemazione delle Missioni tedesche, pp. 35–36, Letter August 10, 1919.

[91] Patrick J. Houlihan, "Renovating Christian Charity: Global Catholicism, the Save the Children Fund, and Humanitarianism during the First World War," *Past & Present* 250, no. 1 (February 2021): 203–241.

Ideologically and pragmatically, the Vatican was well-situated to support famine relief in Eastern Europe, and this caused an unprecedented renovation in Christian charity on behalf of all children regardless of nation or religion. Pope Benedict XV had emerged during the Great War as a credible peace-maker, with condemnations against war emerging in the Autumn of 1914 and concretized in the August 1, 1917 Peace Note, from which Woodrow Wilson had drawn inspiration. Diplomatically shunned by the Great Powers on both sides suspecting that the Church was favoring the enemy, the Catholic Church had freedom of action above state interests at a time unprecedented in the history of the Church since its ancient foundations – also because the Catholic Church existed in a legal gray zone in the period from the unification of Italy until the Lateran Pacts of 1929. A reactionary pope, fuming beneath the self-described martyr's mantle of a "prisoner of the Vatican" because of the unsettled "Roman Question," might have done nothing: The ultimate pater-nalistic and disapproving "I told you so" to the modern world that had led to the Great War's slaughter.

Pope Benedict XV, however, chose to engage contemporary events by offer-ing money and logistical support to those most hurt by war: POWS, displaced persons, widows, and orphans. Personal appeals poured into the Vatican, from Catholics and non-Catholics alike, often begging for money to alleviate the misery that the war had caused. Benedict was besieged with requests, personally approving thousands of requests for money. Benedict XV nearly bankrupted the Vatican's liquidity, which had been drying up as revenue streams diminished in time of war, especially lacking Peter's Pence and the yearly visits of bishops. For the first time in the history of the Catholic Church, the papacy reached out to other faiths (and non-faiths) without demanding conversion or obedience to Rome. The Catholic Church's global network enabled financial sums to be transferred quickly when other channels were unavailable in war-torn Europe. As studies of religious philanthropy and charity have found, individual dona-tions could be potentially overwhelming, which was a reason for more struc-tured, institutionalized giving in the future.

Appeals to Christian charity also reinforced the idea that Western Civilization needed to contain the menace of Bolshevism, which was spread-ing after the Russian Revolution of 1917. With the collapse of the Tsarist state, massive famine in Eastern Europe reigned through the Russian Civil War, with millions of deaths. Thus, donations to Christian charity reaffirmed the bourgeois order of liberal democratic capitalism. The network of soup kitchens became a way to avoid the dangers of anarchy and communism. Benedict intervened to support Save the Children at a crucial moment in the movement's history. Eventually, at the end of the Russian Civil War, the organization had developed mass global appeal and no longer needed the financial or even rhetorical support of the Catholic Church. By 1923, the Great War's disorder had temporarily stabilized.

Global Networks: Between the USA and the USSR, toward Global Civil War

The global networks of humanitarianism reflected the emergence of America as a Great Power, projecting a religiously influenced vision of power in service of liberal democracy against Communism.[92] World War I was the decisive moment in the history of American philanthropy that would have an impact on global history. It caused a restructuring, professionalization, and coordination of apparatuses that had been previously ad hoc.[93] Sometimes written out of modern history dominated by a narrative of secularization, religiously based philanthropic charity would increase throughout the twentieth century, becoming a massive nongovernmental source of humanitarian aid. It helped to solidify American presence in global affairs.

One of these key global networks was the American Jewish Joint Distribution Committee (JDC), founded in 1914. It was led by Juda Magnes, who would become the first Chancellor of Hebrew University and an advocate of a bi-national state of Israel. The AJDC was formed in response to appeals from Jews in Central-Eastern Europe and the Middle East. Another bi-national Israel advocate, Martin Buber, formulated his I-Thou dialectic that stemmed from his recognition of the otherness of Galician Jewish refugees on the streets of Vienna, fleeing the advancing Russian armies in the war's early phase. The so-called *Ostjuden*, or Jews from the *shtetl* of the East, represented a rural way of life completely different from the urbane, assimilationist tendencies of Jews in the metropolitan areas of Central Europe.[94] For Buber, this was a moment of recognition of the Other as an equal partner in a dialectic of human communication. The negative interpretation, however, would perceive this moment of encounter with *Ostjuden* as a moment of fundamental strangeness. The brutal military occupation of Eastern Europe during the First World War brought the German military administrative state into contact with the Jewish Pale of settlement in the Russian Empire. The German military dystopia conceived the need to colonize and civilize a barbaric and strange Eastern realm: with

---

[92] Andrew Preston, *Sword of the Spirit, Shield of Faith: Religion in American War and Diplomacy* (Knopf, 2012).

[93] Robert H. Bremner, *American Philanthropy* (University of Chicago Press, 1960), cited in Cabanes, *The Great War and the Origins of Humanitarianism*, 219.

[94] Paul Mendes-Flohr, *Martin Buber: A Life of Faith and Dissent* (Yale University Press, 2019).

military force if necessary. Such "moments of encounter" would culminate in acts of genocide during the Second World War.[95]

The reordering of the Jewish diaspora community was a key legacy of the First World War, changing migration patterns globally. As Jaclyn Granick has shown for Jewish humanitarianism, this was a process of the Americanization of Jews with the essential assistance of the US government, operating harmoniously in Palestine at the beginning of the war. Neutrality and sectarianism were related concepts.[96] The JDC organized the philanthropic efforts aimed at Jews in Eastern Europe and the Middle East. American Jews represented the largest and wealthiest group of Jews in a neutral country. The American Jewish efforts would play a disproportionate global role with American funding, personnel, and organization proving larger than potential competitors for Jewish philanthropy in the Entente Powers such as Britain and France. As Granick has written, "The JDC maintained almost complete control over all funds raised by American Jews for Jews abroad, making it the most influential of all Jewish philanthropic organizations at the time."[97]

Like other philanthropic organizations, New York City became an important center for the JDC. Especially drawing on the organizing capacities of financiers and lawyers, the JDC channeled these efforts toward political power in Washington, DC, as well as global networks for the distribution of aid to on-the-ground recipients. The JDC was formed to give specific aid to Jews in war-ravaged regions, which American organizers believed would not receive sufficient targeted aid from other sources.[98] In addition to lobbying and writing US government officials to act, personal family connections often proved decisive for getting humanitarian action to its intended recipients. The Warburg brothers, Felix (the head of the JDC in New York) and Max, (the head of the Warburg bank in Hamburg), helped transfer substantial amounts of money raised, even using the US State Department diplomatic pouch for their communications. Having received the monies from the US, Max Warburg would then transfer the monies to a host of Central European Jewish organizations such as the *Hilfsverein der Deutschen Juden*. Before the USA entered the war against the Central Powers in April 1917, the JDC had sent substantial amounts of money to Jews in war-torn East-Central Europe, giving $2.1 million

---

[95] Omer Bartov, *Mirrors of Destruction: War, Genocide, and Modern Identity* (Oxford University Press, 2000); Vejas Gabriel Liulevicius, *War Land on the Eastern Front: Culture, National Identity and German Occupation in World War I* (Cambridge University Press, 2000).

[96] Jaclyn Granick, *International Jewish Humanitarianism in the Age of the Great War* (Cambridge University Press, 2021).

[97] Jaclyn Granick, "Waging Relief: The Politics and Logistics of American Jewish War Relief in Europe and the Near East (1914–1918)," *First World War Studies* 5, no. 1 (2014): 55–68; here, 56.

[98] Granick, "Waging Relief," 55–68.

to Polish Jews and $1.5 to Jews in Austria-Hungary. In Russia before the 1917 Revolution, the JDC, raised another $2.1 million via its channel in St. Petersburg, the Central Jewish Committee for the Relief of Sufferers of War (EKOPO). Arriving on both sides of the conflict, these funds provided essential emergency assistance of food, clothing, and shelter to Jewish civilians, who were sometimes persecuted not only by the enemy but also by the rampaging armies of their own imperial states causing displacement of civilians and a mass crisis of refugees.[99] The Eastern Front in Europe had created an unprecedented type of war with massive fronts that shifted extensively over a wide area, back-and-forth over the course of the war, helping create a crisis of refugee displacement in the wake of shattered empires.

In Palestine and the Ottoman Empire more generally, the US aid to Jews operated differently. The JDC and the Provisional Executive Committee for General Zionist Affairs (PZC) sent relief supplies directly transported by US Navy ships which passed through the blockade imposed by the British and French Navies. The diplomatic arrangements were due to the strong political contacts of American Jews lobbying the Wilson administration. Ambassadors Henry Morgenthau and Abram Elkus were closely affiliated with the JDC. The Jewish journalist Herman Bernstein became a vocal champion of Jewish sectarian relief along with Rabbi Stephen S. Wise.[100] Key connections were forged with influential US policymakers such as Secretary of the Navy, Josephus Daniels. Judeo-Christian values were explicitly enshrined in US military policy on March 15, 1919, when Daniels issued General Order no. 456, which prohibited all forms of unnecessary work on the Christian Sabbath.[101]

Explicit pacifism combined with humanitarianism was a powerful alternative to the carnage of total war. The Society of Friends (Quakers) were religiously motivated actors whose pacifism and conscientious objections influenced their humanitarianism as they opposed military service but through their efforts at care, they nonetheless influenced the social impacts of war on combatants and noncombatants. The US American Friends Service Committee (AFSC) worked with the American Red Cross, which was tasked by Woodrow Wilson with exclusive responsibility for humanitarianism on the battlefield. Even for one religious group, national contexts mattered, with divergent British and American paths regarding how military authorities, skeptical of the Quakers' pacifism, incorporated them within various war-making efforts.[102]

---

[99] Granick, "Waging Relief," 56–57.   [100] Granick, "Waging Relief," 58.
[101] For church-state implications regarding the United States, see Ronit Y. Stahl, *Enlisting Faith: How the Military Chaplaincy Shaped Religion and State in Modern America* (Harvard University Press, 2017).
[102] Salvatici, *A History of Humanitarianism*, 74–75.

Quakerism's pacifist Christian humanitarianism would resonate in a war-torn world. Its nondenominational ecumenism was a counterbalance to rampant secularism and materialism, helping to rally religiously informed idealistic sentiments. In a pamphlet distributed to the League of Nations after a meeting of the International Missionary Council held in Jerusalem from March 24 to April 8, 1928, one of the most influential Quakers of the twentieth century, the American intellectual Rufus M. Jones, wrote a pamphlet, "Christianity and Secular Civilization." Jones argued that "No student of the deeper problems of life can very well fail to see that the greatest rival of Christianity in the world today is not Mohammedanism, or Buddhism, or Hinduism, or Confucianism, but a worldwide secular way of life and interpretation of the nature of things."[103] Jones wrote with a grand view of history, voicing disillusionment with the flashy splendor of the Church, quoting a French prelate visiting Rome from the papacy of Innocent III (1198–1216). Echoing some sentiment from the emerging dialectical theology of Karl Barth and the aspects of the *nouvelle théologie* that would inform the Second Vatican Council (1962–1965), Jones was a historical polemicist for the relevance of the ancient world as a model for contemporary Christianity. In an undated pamphlet entitled, "Our Christian Task in a Materialistic World," he wrote, "Whenever there is a collapse of civilization through an excessive application of the method of strike or lock-out or through a drop down to the barbaric level of trench warfare and high explosives and poison gas, someone always reminds us that Christianity has not failed–it only has not yet been tried! I insist that it has been tried and that it has worked gloriously." Jones stressed the need for humane deeds in living the Christian life, not mere words: "We must, for one thing, as interpreters of Christ, be forever done with gunboat Christianity and with aeroplane-bombing Christianity, and with poison-gas Christianity. We must either stop talking about Christ's ideals of life, or go on talking about them in both word and deed, in the fell clutch of hard facts that may spell death to us, as He did and they did in whose train we want to follow." Jones continued, "There is no other way to build a Christ-like world – no other way except to be Christ-like. We must meet this secular world – its prosperity, its smugness, its 'hard-boiled' philoso-phy, it utilitarian aims – with a settled conviction that we are going all the way through with Christ, and with a burning passion to be like Him in life and spirit – to be His, both to live and to die."[104] Following World War II, Jones traveled to Stockholm to accept the 1947 Nobel Peace Prize awarded to the Quakers.

---

[103] LON, BPC 76/2/19, Rufus M. Jones, "Christianity and Secular Civilization" (Pamphlet) (New York: International Missionary Council, n.d), 5.

[104] LON, BPC 76/2/20, Rufus M. Jones, "Our Christian Task in a Materialistic World," (Pamphlet) (New York: International Missionary Council, n.d.), 5–6.

Before Jones's eventual journey to Stockholm, however, the Quakers would become involved in the Spanish Civil War (1936–1939), a key moment in the globalization of modern war. The Spanish Civil War was a conflict that also did not fit into the paradigm of interwar peace. Along with military interventions, highly politicized humanitarian aid went into a deeply divided Spanish society during extreme situations of civil war, problematizing ideological aid efforts along the political spectrum. The Spanish Civil War became a European civil war, drawing global attention and foreshadowing the destructive events of another world war. Quakers were especially prominent in humanitarian aid in the Spanish Civil War, and as Daniel Maul has shown, the American Quakers, through their central service organization, the American Friends Service Committee (AFSC), played a disproportionate role in providing humanitarian aid because they aided both sides in the conflict. In this acute political conflict of a European civil war, to be on the ground at the sites of humanitarian disaster, Quakers had to articulate and practice a "credible position of both neutrality and impartiality." Maul also argues that the Quakers in the Spanish Civil War had conducted a humanitarian operation that was "essentially secular" in draining out most of the religious content, thus representing a dramatic shift from the Quakers' religiously tinged operations during the First World War.[105]

Marginalized yet Central: The Image of Women and Children

The changing theoretical and practical roles of women in humanitarian work were highly influenced by religious ideals. The legacies and stereotypes of paternalism were strong, representing women as mothers and caregivers, with the Virgin Mary as a key symbol. Nevertheless, the war also saw the emergence of women as public leaders in new professions that fostered female networks of mobility and career advancement. Pioneers like Dorothy Buxton and Eglantyne Jebb advanced new public leadership roles for women, though sometimes circumscribed in paternalistic institutions. Public campaigns for the needs of children reached a major milestone with the Declaration of the Rights of the Child (1924), in the new world forum of the League of Nations. The first three principles declared, "(1) The child must be given the means requisite for its normal development, both materially and spiritually. (2) The child that is hungry must be fed, the child that is sick must be nursed, the child that is backward must be helped, the delinquent child must be reclaimed, and the orphan and the waif must be sheltered and succoured.

---

[105] Daniel Maul, "The Politics of Neutrality – Quaker Relief and the Spanish Civil War 1936–1939," *European Review of History: Revue européenne d'histoire* 23, no. 1–2 (2016): 82–100; here, 82–83, 95.

(3) The child must be the first to receive relief in times of distress."[106] This was a breakthrough moment in the visibility of children's rights in global affairs.

Eglantyne Jebb became the consensus leader of the SCF because she was not seen as a political radical. The SCF's expansion beyond a British local charity became a global international social movement that led to the founding of the Save the Children International Union in Geneva in 1920. After the famine crisis ended in Europe, the SCIU focused on health, education, and child labor conditions, trying to bring up small states in Europe to a perceived common level of civilization. The Declaration of the Rights of the Child became a policy document for the Child Welfare Committee of the League of Nations, represented in the Secretariat, with a focus on Eastern Europe. Avoiding the dilemma of whether the state or the family should take primacy in childcare, the Declaration by aiming for a general proclamation to achieve wide consensus.[107] The Child Welfare Committee was not the direct parent of UNICEF, but it was an ancestor. It provided a base of internationalization and a template for humanitarian aid and associations. The "soup-kitchen" model of relief was highly gendered. At the micro-level, women did most of the distribution work feeding the hungry. Yet they were often in service of organizations that limited women's freedom of action and advancement within the organizations. Famine relief in war became a template for international development at a global level.

In the paternalistic institution that was the Catholic Church in twentieth-century Europe, men held all the prominent leadership roles. Nonetheless, even in the Catholic Church, religious women developed representation and leadership as never before. Madame Florentine Steenbergh-Engheringh was the indefatigable leader of the *Union Internationale des Ligues Feminines Catholiques* (headquartered at Mariaplaats 33 bis, Utrecht) which eventually became the World Union of Catholic Women's Organizations. In the 1920s-1930s, Steenbergh-Engheringh served as the President. She was also part of the Vatican's official section on "women's issues." The Union had been approved in 1913 by Pope Pius X and reconfirmed in 1925 by Pope Pius XI. At the 8th International Congress, held in Rome from May 25–30, 1930, the *Union Internationale* strove to use the "moral grandeur of women" as a basis to "influence public opinion and public authorities so that legislation and social and political institutions are based on the family designed according to the principles of Christian morality."[108] The Rome Congress declared that the

---

[106] Cabanes, *The Great War and the Origins of Humanitarianism,* 248–299.

[107] Salvatici, *A History of Humanitarianism*, 92–93.

[108] ASRS, AAEESS, Stati Eccl. IV Pos. 437 PO, Fasc. 390–397, Unione Internazionale delle Leghe Cattoliche Femminili (UIdLCF) Fasc. 390 pp. 78–90: le VIIIe Conseil International, Rome May 20–25, 1930.

foundation of the family was marriage but with hierarchical leadership and authority: "The man is the head of the family. The woman owes him submission, according to these words of St. Paul: 'The man is the head of the woman, as Christ is the head of the Church, which is His Body and of which he is the Savior.' ... The mother must also devote herself to the care of the home and her children. She is the primary educator of her children."[109] The women's movement included counterrevolutionary and conservative impulses, too, often religiously based.

Visual imagery, and particularly the image of women and children, was an integral part of the nascent international humanitarianism, drawing heavily on religious motives to create mass appeal to virtuous charity. As Heide Fehrenbach and Davide Rodogno have noted, the emergence of the medium of humanitarian photography as a form of mass communication allowed a moral argument to be portrayed visually, where "humanitarian imagery is *moral rhetoric* masquerading as visual evidence."[110] Visual media sought to transcend linguistic and cultural difference, highlighting universal images of suffering, especially that of women and children. Whereas previous humanitarianism during the war had focused on the suffering of soldiers on the battlefield, women and children were the emblematic new civilian sufferers of total war. As seekers of shelter in the Christian narrative of the birth of Christ, Mary and the infant Jesus formed a mainstay of appeals to charity. Continuing the divine aura of relief agencies, sometimes even in secular contexts, Red Cross nurses and female famine relief workers were portrayed in angelic poses, offering aid to the sick, wounded, and malnourished. These depictions allowed donors to believe that their aid contributions were efforts in a just and righteous cause that was advancing the salvation of humanity.

Pandemic, Apocalypse, and Global Awakenings

Many contemporary observers during and after the First World War wondered if the apocalypse was imminent. The influenza pandemic of 1918 became a global moment that reinforced the social nature of systemic change and global interconnectedness influencing public health. Killing between 50 and 100 million people globally, the influenza pandemic of 1918 was a humanitarian crisis, with religious interpretations of a plague as divine retribution that also required

---

[109] ASRS, AAEESS, Stati Eccl. IV, Pos. 437 PO, Fasc. 390–397, Unione Internazionale delle Leghe Cattoliche Femminili (UIdLCF); Fasc. 390, "Union Internationale des Ligues Fem. Cath. Declaration de Principes Prononcée par la Presidente a L'Ouverture du Congres de Rome. May 1930," (booklet), 91.

[110] Heide Fehrenbach and Davide Rodogno, eds., *Humanitarian Photography: A History* (Cambridge, 2015), 6, emphasis in original.

religiously motivated intervention as atonement.[111] Beginning as combat on the Western Front was ending, the flu pandemic would claim more lives than occurred in combat deaths in the war.[112] Following the devastation of war deaths and imperial conquest by the anti-Christ, the humanitarian crises of famine and pestilence completed the symbolic portrait of the Four Horsemen of the Apocalypse, which lent strength to biblical interpretations of prophesied end of the world. The bestselling novel of the First World War was Vicente Blasco Ibáñez's *The Four Horsemen of the Apocalypse* (*Los cuatro jinetes del Apocalipsis*), first published in 1916 and in English translation in 1918. A pop culture phenomenon, the book's filmed version in 1921 also became the break-through feature that launched the career of the film star Rudolph Valentino.[113]

The religious implications of the plague helped reinforce charismatic indigenous preachers whose apocalyptic sermons were tinged with anti-colonial sentiments against Western medicine that seemed powerless to halt the spread of the virus. Asia and Africa, containing most of the world's population, experienced limited battlefield devastation during the First World War. Nevertheless, as European empires collapsed during the twentieth century, the global effects would be felt in the unfolding of anti-colonial nationalism.[114] Africa and Asia would become increasingly important ideologically tinged fields for the politics of humanitarianism.

Especially increasing after 1945, China would become a key battleground for the global ideological sacred-secular battle between Communism and the USA, but major events were already happening because of the First World War.[115] Pope Benedict XV's revolutionary Apostolic Letter of 1919, *Maximum Illud*, was based on missionary experiences in China. Calling for a more balanced and global leadership of the Church befitting the universalistic aims of the faith, *Maximum Illud* called for indigenous clergy to be "co-equal leaders of the Church."[116] The victory of Communism in China caused a further emergence of state-sponsored atheism dominating the political level, while more popular

---

[111] Howard Phillips and David Killingray, eds., *The Spanish Influenza Pandemic of 1918–1919* (Routledge, 2003); Jenkins, *The Great and Holy War*, 181–183.

[112] Kenneth C. Davis, *More Deadly than War: The Hidden History of the Spanish Flu and the First World War* (Henry Holt, 2018). For long-term perspectives of religion and science during pandemics, see Howard Phillips, "'17, '18, '19: Religion and Science in Three Pandemics, 1817, 1918, and 2019," *Journal of Global History* 15, no. 3 (2020): 434–443.

[113] Jenkins, *The Great and Holy War*, 354.

[114] Erez Manela, *The Wilsonian Moment: Self Determination and the International Origins of Anticolonial Nationalism* (Oxford University Press, 2007).

[115] Albert Monshan Wu, *From Christ to Confucius: German Missionaries, Chinese Christians, and the Globalization of Christianity, 1860–1950* (Yale University Press, 2018).

[116] Bryan Lobo, Ilaria Morali, Rolphy Pinto, eds., *Maximum Illud: La Missione Tra Storia e Attualità* (Gregorian & Biblical Press, 2020).

beliefs continued secretly. Even at the official level now, the Vatican continues its concordat diplomacy.[117]

In Africa, the site of the imperialistic scramble that had helped to drag the European empires into the Great War, there were also sites of ideological contestation and conversion. Anti-colonial nationalism, typified by John Chilembewe's revolt in Nyasaland, appealed to religious sensibilities also influenced by charismatic prophets and folk healers. The spread of the pandemic, which followed the trade routes to African seaports, both increased anxieties of doom prophecies as well as undermined legitimacy in Western scientific medicine that did not seem able to stop the virus as a plague. Beyond the pandemic, there were visionary apparitions of vibrant conversions to religion. In Manyikaland, Patrick Kwesha was a missionary who curated a shrine to apparitions of the Virgin Mary, which continued through the 1940s.[118] These Marian visions continued in post-World War II Europe, too, representing a global Catholicism responding to the popular suffering of war and social reordering.[119]

As the famines and pestilence of the war years lessened, religiously oriented humanitarianism temporarily became less visible globally. Its organizational foundations and inspirations remained, however. A wave of NGOs had been established and gained valuable on-the-ground experience, coordinating disparate efforts amid difficult wartime conditions. The Greco-Turkish War ended with the Treaty of Lausanne in 1923, with the Republic of Turkey hardening its borders and denying its responsibility for acts of genocide, something for which the Treaty did not hold Turkey accountable. On a larger scale, the global fighting abated after the end of the Russian Civil War, with the triumph of the Bolsheviks and the solidification of the Soviet Union. With the USA's turn to isolationism in the 1920s, humanitarianism faded as the "Roaring Twenties" generated a period of collective American retreat from the global stage. The "America First" attitude was exacerbated by the new economic crisis of the Great Depression.

The Second World War and Postwar Period: Genocide and "Never Again"?

In contrast to the First World War, when the USA walked away afterward and the USSR was ostracized, the Second World War saw the USA and the USSR as activist global superpowers intervening to determine the contours of world

---

[117] Antonio Spadaro, ed., *Anticipare il futuro della Cina. Ritratto di Mons. Aloysius Jin Luxian S.I.* (Incroci, 2020).

[118] Klaus Koschorke, Frieder Ludwig, and Mariano Delgado, eds., *A History of Christianity in Asia, Africa, and Latin America, 1450–1990: A Documentary Sourcebook* (William B. Eerdmans, 2007), 231–232.

[119] Monique Scheer, *Rosenkranz und Kriegsvisionen: Marienerscheinungskulte im 20. Jahrhundert* (Tübinger Vereinigung für Volkskunde, 2006).

politics both during and after the war. The ideological enmity that had begun during the First World War with the Western liberal fear of Bolshevism had given way to temporary rapprochement during the Second World War as the Allies united against the global threat of Fascism and Nazism. Even before it formally entered the conflict, the USA's massive Lend-Lease program was extended to the Soviet Union in October 1941 after the Nazi invasion of Operation Barbarossa appeared to be winning the war for Hitler's Germany. The united economic and military power of the superpowers during the Second World War defeated the Axis powers. In desperate times, former enemies could aid each other to face an even greater enemy.

In modifying the story of secularization and belief, one of the key links to the study of global humanitarianism in the world wars was the role of the USA and its relation to the USSR. This is particularly true for the ideological dimensions in which religion was a crucial factor and the role of faith-based organizations both inside and outside of governmental structures. As Silvia Salvatici has noted, religion took on a significant role in rehabilitation and reconstruction "because it not only alleviated spiritual suffering but also contributed to the re-acquisition of behavior that was considered healthy and morally correct."[120] The United Nations Relief and Rehabilitation Administration (UNRRA) formally put religious groups at a secondary level, but even so, the indirect influence of faith-based organizations was nevertheless enormous. In the USA, voluntary religious aid exceeded direct government aid.[121] The American vision of religiously influenced humanitarianism was gathering strength that would be unleashed during and after World War II. Learning the lessons of apathy and indifference that had allowed fascism to flourish in the shambles of World War I, during and after World War II, the USA made a more interventionist assertion of its projection of democratic values. Religion was a key part of this, through faith-based charity.

For the history of humanitarianism, a more global view of war helps to rethink the "interwar" era and the history of the Second World War. The era saw the continuation of relief efforts for crises outside the traditional markers of 1918 and 1939. More recent histories of the Second World War have considered the conflict's global and imperial frames beyond Eurocentrism. Especially the expansion of the Japanese Empire, which started before 1914, does not fit the

---

[120] Salvatici, *A History of Humanitarianism*, 130.

[121] Salvatici, *A History of Humanitarianism*, 118; Silvia Salvatici, "Professionals of Humanitarianism: UNRRA Relief Officers in Post-War Europe," in Johannes Paulmann, ed., *Dilemmas of Humanitarian Aid in the Twentieth Century* (Oxford University Press, 2016), pp. 235–262.

standard chronological markers of the world wars, with the start of the Second World War in either 1931 or 1937.[122]

As well as the diplomatic alliances that gave rise to global war, this led to global entanglements of humanitarianism that need further exploration for the period of the Second World War. One such effort was the International Committee for the Nanjing Safety Zone, which helped save people from what would become known as the Nanjing Massacre or "Rape of Nanjing" in 1937–1938. As the invading Japanese Army approached the city, most Westerners fled along with scores of Chinese citizens. A small alliance of determined humanitarians, however, remained to organize emergency efforts. This included businesspeople, journalists, and missionaries: particularly American Protestant missionaries from denominations that included Disciples of Christ, Episcopalians, Methodists, and Presbyterians. The group elected as its leader John Rabe, a Nazi Party member and the CEO of Siemens AG China Corporation, strategically chosen for his global-diplomatic influence that existed because of Nazi Germany's alliance with Imperial Japan in the Anti-Comintern Pact of 1936. The Nanjing humanitarians' safety zone was often a matter of diplomatic delay as the Japanese Army did not stop its advance. The delays, however, were crucial to allow an estimated 250,000 refugees to flee the encroaching destruction, and Rabe became known as the "Schindler of China," personally opening his properties to 650 refugees. Rabe was a complex character, demonstrating both a commitment to Nazism as well as to what scholars have called the "corporate responsibility to protect." In Rabe's words, "at such a time a man tries to behave decently and doesn't want to leave in the lurch the employees under his charge."[123]

The humanitarian networks that developed during the First World War and interwar period provided important international networks and ways of operating. One could continue the story of these humanitarian groups in the Second World War by outlining certain common trends: The need for scientific population management, greater planning, and learned experiences of successes and failures during the previous episodes of famine and disease. The organizations mentioned earlier (Save the Children, YMCA, the Quakers, etc.) continued to develop along these lines during the Second World War. Now they mustered greater resources and applied this in networks that were more global, reflecting

---

[122] For World War II's start date of 1931, see Richard Overy, *Blood and Ruins: The Last Imperial War, 1931–1945* (New York, 2022). For the start date of 1937, see Evan Mawdsley, *World War II: A New History*, 2nd ed. (Cambridge, 2020).

[123] Alain Lempereur, "Humanitarian Negotiation to Protect: John Rabe and the Nanking International Safety Zone (1937–1938)," *Group Decision & Negotiation* 25, no. 4 (July 2016): 663–691; quote from 666.

the wider spread of death and destruction during the Second World War. As important as these efforts were, however, instead of focusing on recounting these efforts in more specific detail, the rest of this Element will spend time focused on selected themes and the global and international effects of humanitarianism.

Expressed in humanitarian terms, the transition from relief to development helped to foreground the complicated relationship between humanitarianism and human rights, especially transitioning between short-term and long-term frameworks. The thoughts and practices of policymakers, activists, and the global public had moments of both continuity and change. As Jessica Reinisch has written, "Importantly, both world wars acted as catalysts in the development of new kinds of relief operations. Although new institutional frameworks and technological solutions were developed during the Second World War, both the design of relief policies and their implementation in actual relief work frequently depended on individuals whose outlooks had been forged in the aftermath of the previous war."[124] For humanitarian policy in World War II, the biggest World War I lesson was that a lack of coordinated international planning was a major problem. Humanitarian organizations' reliance on professional expertise was the biggest distinct change.

Humanitarian aid during and after the Second World War looked to the example of the First World War, both to imitate and to avoid its legacies. First World War relief often happened too little and too late. By contrast, during the Second World War, planning began early during the war itself: It focused on winning the war and controlling the peace. Global disorder due to the First World War had spawned social unrest that caused Communism and Fascism, both ideological enemies that terrified Liberal planners. Indeed, in the post-1945 Liberal consensus, Communism and Fascism were often conflated into the phenomenon of totalitarianism.[125] Learning lessons of World War I, multilateral relief planning was now the order of the day, underpinned by a fervent scientific faith in modern population management techniques, including figures such as John Maynard Keynes and Frederick Leith-Ross.[126] An especially troublesome legacy was Herbert Hoover's insistence that nations pay for the supplies (mostly from USA war food surpluses) or take out debts. Beyond the pressures of the

---

[124] Jessica Reinisch, "Relief in the Aftermath of War," *Journal of Contemporary History* 43, no. 3 (2008): 371–404; here, 392.

[125] Michael Geyer and Sheila Fitzpatrick, eds., *Beyond Totalitarianism: Stalinism and Nazism Compared* (Cambridge University Press, 2009).

[126] Stephen Porter, "Humanitarian Politics and Governance: International Responses to the Civilian Toll in the Second World War," in Michael Geyer and Adam Tooze, eds., *Cambridge History of the Second World War*, 3 vols. (Cambridge University Press, 2015), 3: 502–527; here, 507–508.

wartime economy, especially for nations that lost the war, this exacerbated the economic instability after 1918, helping generate further socio-political disorder. On an intergovernmental level, the League of Nations had received blame for its inadequate protection of minorities and its seeming inability to contain violence.[127]

Geopolitically, Europe had progressed from a position of global domination to global subordination in the emerging superpower contest between the United States and the Soviet Union. As Paul Betts has argued, the irony of the self-appointed European "civilizing" mission was that devasted post-1945 Europe was now a missionary field for civilization to be reestablished in the heart of Europe that had caused so much global destruction.[128] In contrast to the First World War, when the Bolsheviks had been excluded from the Paris 1919 order, humanitarianism was now a global effort, with the involvement of both the new superpowers, the USA and the USSR. There was even some cooperation between the superpowers in the early phases of the post-war era. As it became obvious that the threat of Nazism would be defeated, however, the superpowers' mutual suspicions became stronger, and the transition to the new Cold War increased.

The European Recovery Program, known as the Marshall Plan, became one of the most visible symbols of political economic interventionism for a devastated European continent. As Ian Kershaw has demonstrated in his survey of twentieth century Europe, for all the political symbolism of the Marshall Plan, it addressed one of devastated Europe's crucial economic needs: the dollar deficit. The need for dollar-based aid to stabilize war-torn Europe was an immense problem, and the call for European recovery was real.[129] Post-1945 Europe was a scene of vast migration, and refugees dominated a landscape scarred by war. More recent histories of post-1945 Europe have focused on the great unsettlement as the key condition of the era's rebuilding and reformulations.[130]

The Second World War also foregrounded issues of the legacies of justice in the aftermath of genocide that had caused reflections on the nature of international law, universal jurisdiction, and human rights. One of the key points of analysis of humanitarianism will be the extent to which organizations did or did not intervene to help the unfolding persecution of the Jews and other groups persecuted by the Axis Powers. The processes that became genocide tested the

---

[127] Porter, *Humanitarian Politics and Governance*, 511; see also Ben Shephard, "'Becoming Planning Minded': The Theory and Practice of Relief, 1940–1945," *Journal of Contemporary History* 43, no. 3 (2008): 405–419.

[128] Paul Betts, *Ruin and Renewal: Civilizing Europe after World War II* (Basic Books, 2021).

[129] Ian Kershaw, *To Hell and Back: Europe, 1914–1949* (Penguin, 2015).

[130] Gatrell, *The Unsettling of Europe.*

limits of impartiality and neutrality, which were also key words in judging the actions of Pope Pius XII (1939–1958) and the ICRC.

As events unfolded during World War II, Pope Pius XII was attuned to questions of neutrality, impartiality, and the judgment of history. On January 31, 1943, the same day that the remnants of the German Sixth Army defied Hitler's orders by surrendering at Stalingrad, the pope wrote a letter to Cardinal Michael von Faulhaber of Munich with an eye toward the responsibilities of leadership amid the catastrophe of war. The pope wrote about his special relationship with Munich since his days of diplomatic service as papal nuncio to Bavaria in 1917. Now during the Second World War, Pius XII wrote, "We have defined Our conduct in the face of war with the word 'impartiality,' not with the word 'neutrality.' This could be understood in the sense of passive indifference, an unspeakable attitude for the Supreme Head of the Church in the face of such an event. But the voice of impartiality affirms on Our part a judgment of things according to truth and justice, as far as We have always had every possible regard to the conditions of the Church in the individual states, whenever there were Our public demonstrations; and this in order to spare Catholics from various countries avoidable difficulties." The pope continued, "Precisely by virtue of this impartiality We, as We have repeatedly declared, nurtured the same love for all peoples without exception, since all peoples, each as a whole, have no responsibility at all for the catastrophe that has struck the world."[131]

History will continue to judge the pope's responsibility for acting toward "all peoples without exception," now with much new primary source evidence. With the Vatican archives only opened to historians for the first time in March 2020, historians are beginning to wade through massive amounts of new sources on the role of the Catholic Church during the era of the Second World War and the Holocaust. Historiographical oppositions continue about the so-called "silences" of Pope Pius XII.[132]

Already during the 1930s, the emergence of the increasingly strong Nazi Germany had started to close off avenues of humanitarianism. The Intergovernmental Committee on Refugees (1938) was the wish of President Franklin Roosevelt that reflected a loss of trust in the League of Nations;

---

[131] ASRS, AAEESS, Periodo V, I Parte (1939–1948), Serie: Germania Scatola, Posz. 110, "Minute di lettere del Santo Padre Pio XII in risposta a lettere dei Vescovi Tedeschi 1943–1945," Fascicolo, "Minute di lettere del Santo Padre all'Archivesco di Monaco-Frisinga, Cardinale Michele Faulhaber," 31 Gennaio 1943, pp. 41–45.

[132] After the archival opening in 2020, for early contrasting published views of Pope Pius XII during the Holocaust, see Johan Ickx, *Pio XII e gli ebrei. L'archivista del Vaticano rivela finalmente il ruolo di papa Pacelli durante la Seconda Guerra Mondiale*, trans. Rosa Prencipe, Caterina Chiappa, and Monica Pezzella (Milan, 2021) and David I. Kertzer, *The Pope at War: The Secret History of Pius XII, Mussolini, and Hitler* (Random House, 2022).

however, individual Jewish organizations were successful in facilitating partial escape from the Third Reich.[133] The International Committee of the Red Cross highlighted the symbolic attention that humanitarianism was receiving globally, with the Red Cross winning the Nobel Peace Prize again in 1944, as it had in 1917. The ICRC had knowledge of mass exterminations taking place in Nazi-occupied Europe, yet the ICRC issued no official condemnation, and continued in its plan to take aid to concentration camps. As with other organizations striving for "impartiality" and "neutrality" such as the Catholic Church, the ICRC decided to keep channels open with Nazi Germany. Impartiality and neutrality resulted in "dumb paralysis in the face of the elimination of a people." The rationale was that attempts to intervene with Nazi Germany might have caused greater persecution of all victimized peoples under Nazi control. In opting not to speak out against the persecutions, this also would have completely closed off communication with the Nazi powers. The hope of future continued dialogue and the possibility of improvement later were sublimated theological virtues that proved inadequate in the face of mass extermination. The intolerability of the "suffering of others" had been a core principle of the early foundations of humanitarianism in the modern period, and yet non-Jewish organizations failed to mobilize humanitarian resources to aid the Jews in emergency life-saving relief. In a 2005 commemoration of the Holocaust, the ICRC termed it the "greatest failure in the history of the ICRC."[134] For both sacred and secular organizations, "impartiality" and "neutrality" are key terms in evaluating the nature of genocide and humanitarian interventions.[135]

The most shocking failure of religious humanitarianism, then, became the genocide of the European Jews in the Shoah. The collapse of empires during the First World War had seen the emergence of genocide as a humanitarian rationale for mobilizing world political attention and resources on behalf of the Armenians, a Christian people being exterminated by non-Christian perpetrators. Nevertheless, the better communication channels and developing knowledge of atrocities against Jews during World War II were not enough to overcome the cultural anti-Semitism, failing to mobilize intervention to save non-Christians from destruction by Christian perpetrators. The Nazi Empire was a more formidable military opponent than the weak and ramshackle Ottoman Empire had been. Resistant to outside influence, Hitler's power-hungry

---

[133] Salvatici, *A History of Humanitarianism*, 100.

[134] Quoted in Salvatici, *A History of Humanitarianism*, 122. For the role of the ICRC more long-term, including the place of the Second World War and the Holocaust, see David P. Forsythe, *The Humanitarians: The International Committee of the Red Cross* (Cambridge University Press, 2005); Neville Wylie, Melanie Oppenheimer and James Crossland, eds., *The Red Cross Movement: Myths, Practices and Turning Points* (Manchester University Press, 2020).

[135] Donald Bloxham, *History and Morality* (Oxford University Press, 2020).

pan-European Nazi Empire was implacable and had to be militarily crushed before the humanitarian relief effort effectively could aid the populations in need. The Jewish networks that had mobilized enormous resources of money and material aid to their fellows in Eastern Europe and the Middle East during the First World War also could not sufficiently motivate their own governments to intervene quickly and forcefully enough to save Jews in peril in Hitler's Europe.

This egregious failure of humanitarian intervention during the Holocaust has since become the symbolic low point for assessing a human-caused disaster consciously inflicted by one population on another. As well as the key activism of justifiably outraged Jewish networks that mobilized effectively in the international diplomatic climate of the new United Nations, Western guilt for the destruction of European Jews underlay Western support for the creation of the State of Israel in 1948, seen by many Palestinians and Arabs as the *Nakba* (disaster).[136] At a focal point of global conflict in world history, the new state of Israel demonstrated a tragic paradox of humanitarian relief: An effort to alleviate the suffering of one group of people created suffering for another group of people.

UNRRA: A Temporarily United Global Relief Effort

The United Nations Relief and Rehabilitation Administration (UNRRA) was symbolic of how far the global humanitarian order had progressed in its planning and international cooperation, blending idealism and realism to adapt to new global challenges. In the words of President Franklin Delano Roosevelt, the UNRRA would be the "humanitarian arm" of the Grand Alliance. As Elisabeth Borgwardt has argued, this was an expansive vision of a "New Deal for the world."[137] Herbert H. Lehman became the Director of the UNRRA in 1944, and he formed his leadership perspectives based on his experiences with the JDC in World War I.[138]

The United Nations Relief and Rehabilitation Administration established in November 1943 was the largest and most important international humanitarian organization in terms of the impact of its operations and the influence of its ideas, either before or since. Between 1944 and 1947, it spent almost $4 billion, providing aid for 20 million war victims in 16 formerly Axis-dominated countries in Europe, East Asia, and Africa. It grew to include 20,000 employees

---

[136] Eric D. Weitz, *A World Divided: The Global Struggle for Human Rights in the Age of Nation-States* (Princeton University Press, 2019), 320–367.

[137] Elizabeth Borgwardt, *A New Deal for the World: America's Vision for Human Rights* (The Belknap Press, 2005).

[138] Salvatici, *A History of Humanitarianism*, 116–117.

from 50 countries, and its 48 member states represented 80 percent of the world's population. The large scope of the operations, however, understated the extent of UNRRA because civil society voluntary agencies provided personnel and material aid under the UNRRA's remit. Drawing on pre-WWII roots, many of these civil society institutions were religious in nature, especially given the high degree of religious-natured giving in the USA and the dominance of the USA in postwar planning.[139] UNRRA tried to relegate religious organizations to a secondary level, but in the USA voluntary religious aid exceeded government aid. However, even organizations that were secularizing, like UNRRA, had leaders who were formed by religious humanitarianism in the First World War. Religion was an inescapable part of the world wars' legacy.[140]

Despite just criticisms of selective intervention, the UNRRA made a difference in life or death for millions. In the words of Grace Fox, a contemporary observer and scholar, the UNRRA provided the "first blueprint of the postwar order."[141] Vitally, it kept populations alive and healthy, which allowed shattered states time to focus on rebuilding their societies. Thus, the UNRRA as an institution was vital for the transition from emergency relief to development. By providing "short-term stability" in "dangerously unstable environments" it allowed "political rejuvenation and diplomatic engagement."[142]

The multilateral UNRRA was a major achievement, especially in contrast to the First World War, when the Bolsheviks were excluded, and the USA renounced participation in the League of Nations. Planning began during the Second World War. After Soviet plans for spheres of influence in individual countries were diminished, small-group diplomacy worked through controversies. However, the UNRRA was a Great Power affair in its leadership, with a Central Committee. The USA predominated due to its socio-economic output, producing one-half of the world's industrial output in 1945; the USA was the largest contributor of money and material. In contrast to how the Wilson administration alienated Republicans in the Senate leading them to derail US participation in the League of Nations, the UNRRA was styled as a patriotic effort to win the peace and the Truman administration successfully courted Congressional Republicans to support the efforts at humanitarian international diplomacy.[143] By 1947, the UNRRA wound down as the Cold War began in earnest. The idea of forced repatriation to Soviet spheres of influence in Eastern

---

[139] Porter, "Humanitarian Politics and Governance," 503–507. For the official history of UNRRA, see George Woodbridge, *UNRRA: The History of the United Nations Relief and Rehabilitation Administration*, 3 vols. (Columbia University Press, 1950).

[140] Salvatici, *A History of Humanitarianism*, 117–119; McCleary, *Global Compassion*, 36–59

[141] Quoted in Porter, "Humanitarian Politics and Governance," 507.

[142] Porter, "Humanitarian Politics and Governance," 524.

[143] Porter, "Humanitarian Politics and Governance," 516.

Europe led Congress to withdraw funding. Except for specific United Nations refugees, the ICRC and civil society organizations assumed war relief in the Cold War and beyond.[144]

The Second World War's legacies were formed by the experience of the First World War but went beyond it. The international framework offered protection to refugees and minorities beyond the efforts of the League of Nations, the Nansen offices, and Western-based civil society organizations such as the International Labor Organization. The UNRRA's successor organization was the International Refugee Organization (IRO), which was dissolved in 1952. UNRRA and IRO personnel, planning, and resources were given to the World Health Organization, and the UN High Commissioner for Refugees (1951–present).[145]

The UNRRA began in 1943, even before the outcome of the Second World War was decided. As Jessica Reinisch has argued, key historical lessons of the previous war combined with projections for the new global order.[146] In the immediate aftermath of the Second World War, humanitarianism was still Eurocentric but rapidly becoming global. Humanitarian efforts in Europe focused on relief, moving toward long-term reconstruction and rebuilding. Globally outside of Europe, the humanitarian internationalist focus initially was on relief, but over time this changed to ideas about development. This became a tricky, unanswerable question: Did development mean developing indigenous frameworks, utilizing Eurocentric blueprints, administering supposedly neutral or value-free criteria, or creating a complicated synthesis of these options?

The new global order included the Soviet Union, but world humanitarianism was still dominated by the United States and the neo-liberal order centered in Anglo-American politics. The UNRRA, for example had an initial budget of $3.7 billion, of which the United States provided $2.7 billion, with Britain and Canada providing most of the remainder. The USA provided around 73 percent of UNRRA's funds over the course of its existence.[147] UNRRA's operations were bureaucratically centered in New York, officially becoming part of the United Nations in 1945 and largely ceasing operations in 1947. The UNRRA became essential for reconstructing postwar Europe, especially managing the

---

[144] Porter, "Humanitarian Politics and Governance," 524.

[145] Porter, "Humanitarian Politics and Governance," 523–24.

[146] Jessica Reinisch, "'We Shall Rebuild Anew a Powerful Nation': UNRRA, Internationalism and National Reconstruction in Poland," *Journal of Contemporary History* 43, no. 3 (2008): 451–476; Jessica Reinisch, "Auntie UNRRA at the Crossroads" *Past & Present* 218, no. 8 (2013): 70–97; Jessica Reinisch, "Internationalism in Relief: The Birth (and Death) of UNRRA," *Past & Present* 210, no. 6 (2011): 258–289.

[147] McCleary, *Global Compassion*, 65.

relocation of people that included displaced persons and refugees, unsettled by the Second World War. The vastness of the problem was a challenge that met with immense success.

After UNRRA

After the Second World War, civil society humanitarian endeavors flourished as non-state voluntary agencies expanded rapidly. The US State Department organized the largest and most professional organizations into the American Council of Voluntary Agencies. The Council was controlled by the War Relief Board and administered by the US State Department, which exercised a quality control function to consolidate and reduce the number of relief agencies. The Council consisted of forty-eight organizations, many of which had religious affiliations such as the American Jewish Joint Distribution Committee, the Young Men's Christian Association (YMCA), and the American Friends.[148]

The American Council of Voluntary Agencies for Foreign Service was the precursor organization to what became known as CARE, the Cooperative for American Remittances to Europe that shifted its name to Cooperative for Assistance and Relief Everywhere. This was the organization responsible for the famous CARE packages, symbolic of tangible aid to feed starving people.[149] This umbrella federation was part of a nexus of governmental and nongovernmental aid, sometimes arranged in a hybrid fashion, with civil society organizations subject to governmental regulations, in what has been called an "NGO revolution."[150]

Religious organizations grounded in America were vital parts of this trend. For Protestants, Bob Pierce turned World Vision International into the world's largest Christian humanitarian organization in the world with 42,000 employees, offices in over 100 countries, and an annual budget of over $2 billion.[151] The American Jewish Relief Committee continued its upward trajectory of financial support, though the post-1945 world faced a radically changed global landscape in the aftermath of the Shoah and the creation of the State of Israel.

The religious charity of Catholic Relief Services (CRS) was one of the untold economic ideological histories of the post-1945 era as a humanitarian organization rebuilding a devastated world. Catholic Relief Services became another crucial part of the reenergized landscape of religiously influenced humanitarian

---

[148] Salvatici, *A History of Humanitarianism,* 123–124; McCleary, *Global Compassion,* 36–59.

[149] Heike Wieters, *The NGO CARE and Food Aid from America, 1945–80: "Showered with Kindness"?* (Manchester University Press, 2020).

[150] Porter, "Humanitarian Politics and Governance," 525–526; Woodbridge et al., *UNRRA,* 2: 67–78.

[151] King, *God's Internationalists.*

aid.[152] The organization was officially founded in 1943, and its own institutional history stressed the prior experience of the First World War. This was particularly so for the National Catholic War Council in 1917, which was the first time that American bishops had sponsored the first nationwide association of American Catholics, leading to the founding of the National Catholic Welfare Council in 1919.[153] As it was officially founded in 1943, CRS was an initiative of US bishops that formed a core component of US NGOs in World War II and the postwar era. Throughout most of Pope Pius XII's reign, CRS was known as War Relief Services of the National Catholic Welfare Conference (or War Relief Services; its name officially changed to Catholic Relief Services in 1955 but CRS will be used here to stress the more familiar name). Catholic Relief Services was a wartime emergency measure that turned into a huge multi-billion-dollar relief and development organization.

Catholic Relief Services was originally smaller in numbers of personnel and funds than the organizations of American Protestants and Jews, but Catholics had many philanthropic initiatives in disparate countries. Catholic Relief Services was an effort to centralize national and global measures that would also look after local concerns, beginning with Polish diaspora aid following the invasion of Poland in 1939. In the words of Salvatici, CRS "became the most important US non-governmental agency in the post-Second-World-War era."[154] The only published book conveying the institutional history of CRS was written by a key former practitioner, Eileen Egan, and it was a book of passionate institutional advocacy grounded in personal experience. Egan's work documented the foundational institutional history of CRS. Filled with colorful vignettes and a basic institutional narrative arc, Egan's book helped to flesh out many people who became leading figures in CRS. The book, however, was highly selective: focusing on "success" stories and insufficiently self-critical of the institution, with difficulties usually attributed to outside organizations or generic circumstances. Egan's account remained silent about behind-the-scenes disputes, power struggles, and compromises: both internal to CRS as well as to the complex decision-making in the Vatican and the US government.

The history of CRS took shape during emergency war measures. The American government made efforts to organize disparate agencies through the War Relief Control Board (WRCB) in July 1942. In the Catholic case, this involved the Bishops' War Emergency and Relief Committee, which was licensed by the WRCB. This generated a plethora of local Community Chests and Councils. It created a national budget for war appeals. The emergency relief

---

[152] Eileen M. Egan, *Catholic Relief Services: The Beginning Years* (Catholic Relief Services, 1988), 1–24.
[153] Egan, *Catholic Relief Services*, 3   [154] Salvatici, *A History of Humanitarianism,* 122–123.

measures had some parallels with measures in the First World War, which the existing literature has not investigated in sufficient detail. In the Autumn of 1942, the WRCB decided to create the National War Fund, as a "single joint appeal to the American community for all needs relating to the war." On January 15, 1943, the Administrative Board of the Bishops' War Emergency and Relief Committee decided to participate in this broad nationwide appeal by creating a Catholic overseas aid agency distinct from the Bishops' War Emergency and Relief Committee (which was limited to the religious care of Catholic needy). The new Catholic overseas agency was to provide aid based on need alone. Catholic Relief Services' operational headquarters were to be in New York City to be close to refugee arrivals, warehouses, and overseas relief shipping lines. In Egan's words, "Its aim was to extend help to war-afflicted people, especially children, on the basis of need alone, without reference to race, creed, or other factors."[155]

The first programs of CRS were included in the National War Fund Appeal in Autumn 1943. The nationwide goal was $125 million, and the American people gave $126 million. The amount allocated to CRS was $2,370,000: for health, welfare, and relief activities, as distinguished from church or religious activities. Purely religious needs were to be funded by Bishops' War Emergency and Relief Committee. Special arrangements for countries were to be channeled through agencies of countries concerned, for example, French relief programs were transferred by the National War Fund to American Relief for France and then to CRS. Catholic Relief Services operated with the National War Fund through the fall campaign of 1946. In 1947, CRS appealed directly to Catholic people on Laetare Sunday in Lent, merging its appeal with Bishops' War Emergency and Relief Collection. The Catholic community donated nearly $8 million to this appeal.[156]

Catholic Relief Services was a case study of how relief transitioned into development, but this process remained unclear. In contrast to other Catholic charities grounded in helping the poor in national contexts since the nineteenth century or earlier, CRS was a transnational wartime emergency measure focused on helping refugees and migrants who had been devastated because of World War II. It was part of the story of American global involvement in European affairs and the displacement of European global hegemony. However, what began as emergency war relief transitioned, and CRS's mandate evolved into something more long-term: now focused on global development politics. Historians partially do not know how this process of evolution happened because it occurred in the 1940s–1950s, a period for which the Vatican Archives were closed to all researchers until 2020, also complicated by the need to access CRS's archival records.

---

155 Egan, *Catholic Relief Services*, 14–16.   156 Egan, *Catholic Relief Services*, 16–17.

There is much work to be done on the vital role of Catholic women in sustaining CRS as donors and as workers. Women were marginalized from leadership positions from most of the hierarchical positions of power in the Church's patriarchy. However, in the paternalistic ideology that confined women to roles as mothers and minders of the family, women were central to the church's ideology of "organic" family values, with the example of the Virgin Mary as the Mother of Jesus as a cornerstone of the faith. The hypocrisy of the Church on the role of women concealed another interesting social fact about the Church's operations: Women (both religious and lay) were the primary historical agents of working for and distributing humanitarian aid, both domestically at the parish level and internationally through the emergence of NGOs. It was women who worked the soup kitchens, cared for orphan children, and helped refugees find a home. The gendered dimensions are fundamental to understanding modern humanitarianism, yet they have only recently started to be theorized and researched by modern historians.[157] Thus, a major aim of future research is to remedy a gender imbalance in Catholic history, bringing to light the unknown and hidden stories of the women who did most of the humanitarian work. Correcting a historiographical imbalance that focuses on the patriarchy of religious leadership, this would be a "family" history of Catholic humanitarians that gives women their equal place in the modern history of religion. Recognition of CRS and the role of women in the history of humanitarianism is long overdue.

Catholic Relief Services, in its early formation phase from 1943 until the 1950s, thus occupies a crucial point of transition in the politics of relief changing to development, ideally situated to analyze humanitarianism and human rights. The public history of CRS is quickly stated in brief mission statements on the CRS website, where the organization declares, "We are the official overseas relief and development agency of the United States Conference of Catholic Bishops and a member of Caritas Internationalis."[158] Even in this short statement, the tensions between relief and development are not resolved, and the main historical question remains unanswered of how the mandate evolved from relief into development policy. Founded in the USA in 1943 and growing from nothing, CRS became a multi-billion-dollar organization involved in global development, crucial for understanding the modern history of Europe and the United States in the reshuffling of the global order in the Cold War.

---

[157] Esther Möller, Johannes Paulmann, and Katharina Stornig, eds., *Gendering Global Humanitarianism in the Twentieth Century: Practice, Politics and the Power of Representation* (Palgrave, 2020).

[158] www.crs.org/about/crs-history accessed on July 8, 2022.

Extant scholarship on CRS is limited in viewpoint, and often in terms of advocacy or condemnation. Humanitarian organizations are often uninterested in their own long-term history, preferring to focus their institutional efforts on the contemporary day-to-day needs and plans of the organization. Thus, a key research aim is a critical history of this major development organization. Catholic Relief Services's archives are part of historical records that involve global and local political issues, relating to questions of access and disclosure, which also impact the methodology and viewpoints about religious humanitarianism.

The history of humanitarianism in the post-1945 era is a work of contemporary history currently in progress. Because of this, political and logistical questions continue to influence current decision-making and access to historical records. Issues of data protection, privacy, and the avoidance of controversy can influence what historical materials are available to researchers. Catholic Relief Services, for instance, at one time made part of its records in Baltimore freely accessible to the public, and there are movements to re-open access to the records. In a 1993 newsletter of the Cushwa Center at the University of Notre Dame, the archivist, Sister Rosalie McQuade wrote, "CRS Archives Library Research Records Center is open from 9:00 a.m. to 5:00 p.m. Monday through Friday. Researchers are asked to make an appointment to use the collections. Kindly address correspondence or phone calls to: Rosalie McQuaide, CSJP, Archivist Historian and Records Manager."[159] Times change, archivists change, funding priorities change, and organizations must make tough decisions about how much of their records to keep open, especially as these records continue to the present day. Even a hierarchical organization like the Catholic Church has different power centers in Rome and the USA. The problem of opening Catholic archival records is a complex matter, inflamed by the contemporary politics of such issues as the ongoing clerical sexual abuse scandal and the legacy of the Church's actions during and after the Holocaust.

The questions of the Holocaust and its legacy are crucial for assessing humanitarianism in the twentieth century. By officially opening the Vatican records of the pontificate of Pope Pius XII in March 2020, the Vatican made a decisive step toward dealing with the historical record of a controversial pope during the Second World War and the events of the Holocaust. In making this decision, Pope Francis declared, "The Church is not afraid of History."[160] Trapped in contemporary polemics about Pius XII's alleged anti-Semitism or cause for sainthood, the historical verdict on Pius XII will not be "settled" by

---

[159] Cushwa Center for the Study of American Catholicism, "Archives," *American Catholic Studies Newsletter* 20, no. 2 (Fall 1993): 10–12.

[160] www.reuters.com/article/us-pope-archives-idUSKCN1QL11Q accessed July 8, 2022.

historical consensus anytime soon. Humanitarian history often seeks to personify complex processes, reduced to a single figure of identification. The temptation for personalized definitive judgment is strong, especially about the symbolic leader of the Catholic Church during the Second World War, Pope Pius XII. From the extant archival disclosures, there is not likely to be a Nixonian moment of "What did he know? And when did he know it?" that will definitively change opinions and settle the question of Pius XII's personal degree of complicity for his actions or inactions about the unfolding events of the Holocaust.

Especially in public debate, interpretations of Pius XII quickly descend into hypothetical (sometimes even counterfactual) polemics that represent moral and ethical questions rather than historical ones: What could he or what should he have done? By contrast, more informed scholarly historical accounts will bring contextualization that will help scholars and the public interpret fundamental questions of continuity and change, especially through the world wars. History's collective verdict on Pope Pius XII is still being formed, and this will continue for a long time in the future. To unpack the questions of Catholic modernity between the nineteenth century and the era of the Second Vatican Council, scholars need to reassess the era of the world wars. There is much work to be done, and one must be skeptical of historians who claim to have the definitive historical verdict of the legacy of Pope Pius XII.

Polemics about Pope Pius XII often reduce the agency of the Catholic Church to the figure of the pope and the centralized, hierarchical Vatican bureaucracy. Instead, there is a need for a broader and deeper nuanced examination of historical agency in the study of humanitarianism – and for viewing the Catholic Church in its global and transnational contexts. Historical judgment proceeds inexorably, with room for revision and debate. Humanitarian organizations like Catholic Relief Services that operate under the umbrella of Catholic authority must recognize that silences can be suspect.

Global Mission and Development: Colonialism Continued?

Africa, the so-called "Dark Continent," was indeed a site of savagery by non-Africans visiting violence and oppression on native African populations. In the pre-1914 world, European empires exerted global hegemony through their economic empires, backed up with military power. The so-called "scramble for Africa" helped to bring European empires into diplomatic confrontations that resulted in the outbreak of the First World War. In North Africa and Asia, Europeans and Americans constructed their own "civilized" identity by othering a vision of patronizing exotic Orientalism. Sub-Saharan Africa received an even more brutal, de-humanizing othering, with modern episodes of genocide of peoples such as the Herero and Namaqua.[161]

The historical experiences, voices, and thoughts of native Africans represent some of the most pivotal and yet most elusive topics for historical research in humanitarianism and the struggle for human rights. The path-breaking work of Bonny Ibhawoh has helped to call attention to the issue that, "In Africa, where the nation-state has had the shortest history, national identities remain fragile and unsettled."[162] Ibhawoh argues that the modern nation-state framework is particularly inappropriate to view the story of human rights in Africa because of the triumphalist and linear teleological narratives that focus on the twentieth century and particularly the post-1945 period. Considering the global ruptures and reordering through the twentieth century to the present, this conception includes both North Africa and Sub-Saharan Africa. Ibhawoh argues for a complex history that stresses continuity and change over the long-term narrative of "indigenous Africans rights traditions" with deep roots prior to 1914. Instead of a neat morality tale of "ruthless violators and benevolent protectors," Ibahwoh's work represents a spectrum of diverse actors including the traditional wisdom of elders and sages (along with warriors and monarchs), new interactions with non-African humanitarians and abolitionists, native populations and their would-be colonizers (including those who bent on enslaving and exterminating natives), nationalists and anti-colonists, as well as dictators and dissidents.[163] Non-African populations struggled to understand Africa, mobilizing resources to respond to humanitarian emergencies, which continue to the present day. In March 1968, Africa Concern came to Dublin, trying to translate the reality of the starvation and suffering of the Biafran Civil War in Nigeria by mobilizing a coalition of missionaries, volunteers, and others to try to create a "people to people" approach, coordinating private agencies, raising awareness, and mobilizing public responses.[164]

Through the violence of the twentieth century, African indigenous traditions have much to teach about the struggle for human rights, including the idea of dignity. As a formative philosophical concept, dignity has united human rights thinkers as an organizing principle for conceptualizing human rights. Perhaps most famously articulated through Archbishop Desmond Tutu as part of the public hearings of the South African Truth and Reconciliation Commission

---

[161] A. Dirk Moses, *Empire, Colony, Genocide: Conquest, Occupation and Subaltern Resistance in World History* (Berghahn Books, 2008).

[162] Bonny Ibhawoh, *Human Rights in Africa* (Cambridge University Press, 2018), xiv.

[163] Ibhawoh, *Human Rights in Africa*, xii. For the deep roots of traditional wisdom, see Ibhawoh, *Human Rights in Africa*, esp. 30–54.

[164] Salvatici, *A History of Humanitarianism*, 188. See also Kevin O'Sullivan, *The NGO Moment: The Globalisation of Compassion from Biafra to Live Aid* (Cambridge University Press, 2021).

(TRC), the idea of *Ubuntu*, a Bantu word meaning "humanity" (sometimes translated as "I am because we are") represented a fundamental relational reciprocity. In Tutu's words, "My humanity is caught up in your humanity, and when your humanity is enhanced – whether I like it or not – my humanity is enhanced. Likewise, when you are dehumanized, inexorably, I am dehumanized as well."[165]

Africa needs to receive much further historical attention for the historical and contemporary implications of humanitarianism and human rights. In the context of publishing limits, the present work regrettably can devote only limited space to the issue here, but historians are taking up the challenge, showing how African history is reshaping global history and awareness. Elizabeth Foster's superb work on Catholicism's complex role in African decolonization is only one exemplary effort. The indigenization of clerical leadership, articulated by Pope Benedict XV in *Maximum Illud*, was a delayed project that gained strength after the Second World War, especially in the era after the Second Vatican Council. As Foster has shown for Francophone Africa, the most prominent colonial power exerting Catholic influence in a complicated church-state relationship, as late as 1952, there were only 180 African clergy members in the lands of French West Africa, French Equatorial Africa, French Togo, and French Cameroon, while the number of European, mostly French clergy was 1,096.[166] Before the Great War, the Vatican and the French state had officially severed diplomatic relations because of *laïcité* laws of 1904–1905. French Catholic missionaries would continue to be agents of the French empire, with mission churches and schools serving as formative grounds for enculturating European religious values in African peoples. The process of enculturation, however, was complex and multi-faceted, with cultural influence proceeding in different directions between centers and peripheries. Even within the Catholic Church, there were tensions between support for old colonial structures as well as movements for decolonization and independence. In the present day, when European vocations to the priesthood are declining, non-Europeans are becoming increasingly influential in shaping the theory and practice of the Catholic Church in the modern world.[167]

The atheistic state powers were also involved in the global struggle for hearts and minds in the post-1945 world. Following the defeat of communist revolutions in the era from 1917–1923, the Soviet Union under Stalin had turned inward to a policy of "Socialism in One Country," thus temporarily postponing

---

[165] Quoted in Ibhawoh, *Human Rights in Africa*, 31–32.

[166] Elizabeth A. Foster, *African Catholic: Decolonization and the Transformation of the Church* (Harvard University Press, 2019),156.

[167] McGreevy, *Catholicism*.

the Marxist theory of the interdependent world revolution of Communism. Concentrating on building the USSR, the horrors of Stalinism had restructured Soviet society on a massive scale unprecedented in world history. Stalin's near-fatal mistake of a temporary alliance with Nazi Germany had almost resulted in the extinction of the Soviet experiment during World War II. The Soviet Union, deeply shaken by massive destruction and death on an unimaginable scale during the war, began massive rebuilding efforts. As the USSR stabilized, Soviet policy became more global again. Soviet control of Eastern Europe created a security buffer zone against the fear of future Western military invasions. Globally, the Soviet Union became involved in a power contest with the USA, with both sides trying to control vast spheres of influence. As state-sponsored atheism became involved again in global policy on a grand scale, vast humanitarian projects throughout the world were a vital part of the effort. Socialist powers intervened in world affairs to influence public health, anti-famine aid, vaccination campaigns, and a panoply of humanitarian causes now bound up with development but with a noncapitalist rationale.[168]

These developments had legacies that continue, and the ideological aspects of global policy deserve further study. The Global South, both quantitatively and qualitatively, is a geopolitical social fact that must inform any assessment of religious humanitarianism in the contemporary era. Referring to the socially encompassing presence of religion in the (European) Middle Ages, Philip Jenkins, a leading scholar of global religious developments, argues that the imminent "next Christendom" will be outside Europe, with centers in the Americas, Africa, and Asia. There will be a decidedly non-European center of gravity in a contemporary world that also redevelops ancient roots.[169] The stunning growth of new converts to Christianity (and Islam, for that matter), counters simplistic notions of a Euro-centric narrative of global secularization. From the data gathered by the Center for Global Christianity, the World Christian Database, estimates that by 2030, Africa will be the world's largest Christian continent.[170] The vibrant new religious converts have led to large demographic increases in Christian believers, shifting most believers to the Global South. Serious scholarship on the global effects of the world wars must consider the broader global story of religious change. The story of Global Christianity, the Abrahamic faith that predominates in Western liberal

---

[168] James Mark et al., *Socialism Goes Global: The Soviet Union and Eastern Europe in the Age of Decolonisation* (Oxford University Press, 2022).

[169] Philip Jenkins, *The Next Christendom: The Coming of Global Christianity*, 3rd ed. (Oxford University Press, 2011).

[170] Todd M. Johnson and Gina A. Zurlo, eds. *World Christian Database* (Brill, 2023). Based at the Center for Global Christianity, see the World Christian Database, https://worldchristiandatabase.org; accessed December 8, 2023.

awareness of the extent of religion in politics, must also be balanced by awareness of non-Christian elements: not only the Abrahamic faiths of Judaism and Islam but also a plurality of religious faiths as well as the secularists subscribing to no religious faith whatsoever. Global Christianity changed from a Eurocentric global hegemon to one faith among many, with its power centers outside of Europe.[171]

The reassertion of religious identities for contemporary global humanitarianism defies secularist normative presumptions. Created in 1984 in England as a response to aid the humanitarian crises in Ethiopia and Sudan, Islamic Relief is one of the best-known agencies, rapidly transforming into one of the biggest Islamic aid agencies known to the West, from modest beginnings and aims to a huge global presence with an annual budget of $109 million (not including monies raised by local branches).[172] The politics of the Global "War on Terror" in the aftermath of the terrorist attacks of 2001 have caused mutual suspicion and incomprehension as multiple parties across the globe try to derive meaning from ideas of the proper role of Muslim charities and their relation to institutions of mosques and madrasas. Regarding the constant rearticulation of sacred and secular, as Cecilia Lynch has argued, "religious ethics and action in a secular world, or secular ethics and action in a religious world, are constitutive constructs. They rework each other constantly, but the intersection of local contexts with global discourses and practices, including those of the 'war on terror' and the liberal market, produces trends that can be identified and analyzed."[173]

In the global history of ideological humanitarianism, non-European and non-American peoples must be considered in regimes of power, looking at complex relationships of subordination and domination. Non-Europeans and non-American peoples are increasingly in positions of influence, sometimes even as hegemons helping to shape global history. Consider the case of the emergence of modern China and its implications for a history of ideological humanitarianism in the modern era.

---

[171] Todd M. Johnson and Kenneth R. Ross, eds., *Atlas of Global Christianity* (University of Edinburgh Press, 2009). For the long-term implications, see Diarmaid MacCulloch, *A History of Christianity: The First Three Thousand Years* (Viking, 2009).

[172] Michael Barnett and Janice Gross Stein, "Introduction: The Secularization and Sanctification of Humanitarianism," in Michael Barnett and Janice Gross Stein, eds., *Sacred Aid: Faith and Humanitarianism* (Oxford University Press, 2012), 6. On the role of Islamic charities more generally, see M. A. Mohamed Salih, "Islamic NGOs in Africa: The Promise and Peril of Islamic Voluntarism," in Alex de Waal, ed., *Islamism and Its Enemies in the Horn of Africa* (Bloomington: Indiana University Press, 2004), 146–181.

[173] Cecelia Lynch, "Religious Humanitarianism and the Global Politics of Secularism," in Craig Calhoun, Mark Juergensmeyer, and Jonathan van Antwerpen, eds., *Rethinking Secularism* (Oxford University Press, 2011) 204–224; here, 204–205.

In humanitarian terms, the history of China is remarkable and utterly transformative. China was a mission field in the pre-1914 era, heavily controlled by European and American powers. Having gone through twentieth-century war and revolutions, China is now a global superpower and the world's most populous country. In a comparatively brief time, China has undergone a development unprecedented in human history.[174] At the beginning of the twentieth century, the corruption of the authoritarian Qing dynasty could not address the mass suffering of famine, rebellions, and war, complicated by foreign military interventions. Chinese philanthropists helped to develop a model of the Chinese Red Cross that drew on existing alliances.[175] As Miwa Hirono argues, China's humanitarian model is still not well understood in terms of its grounding in a well-ordered state (and its sometimes-anti-Western feelings) based on comprehensive human-oriented development in which traditional Confucianism is a major ideological source.[176] Ironically, through the intertwining of economic interests, one could argue that China is now helping to restructure the West. Vast issues of mutual incomprehension and suspicion remain about China and its relations with the West.[177]

Exploration and development continue globally, and ideological humanitarianism will continue to be a part of these actions. Human exploration continues in a process of "discovery" that evokes historical comparisons to the seaborne Age of Empires. Some of the new frontiers announced are the Arctic and Antarctic regions, contested over territoriality and resources. Driven by processes of global anthropocentric climate change, these "unsettled" regions are becoming more accessible to human exploration and even habitation.[178]

The search for habitable environments and resources has escaped the limits of Earth. The exploration and missionary impulses that motivated European seafarers in the age of "discovery," and influenced concepts of humanitarianism and human rights during the Atlantic slave trade, have been reloaded. Space as the "final frontier" is no longer a preserve of science fiction; space is now a contested field for ideologically framed exploration that includes

---

[174] The literature on this process is enormous. For an overview on the cusp of the 1949 Communist Revolution, see Jack Neubauer, "Adopting Revolution: The Chinese Communist Revolution and the Politics of Global Humanitarianism," *Modern China* 47, no. 5 (2021): 598–627.

[175] Yannan Li, "Red Cross Society in Imperial China, 1904–1912: A Historical Analysis," *Voluntas* 27 (2016): 2274–2291.

[176] Miwa Hirono, "Three Legacies of Humanitarianism in China" *Disasters* 37, Supplement 2 (October 2013): S202–S220.

[177] For an introduction to this vast theme, see Rana Mitter and Elsbeth Johnson, "What the West Gets Wrong about China," *Harvard Business Review* 99, no. 3 (2021): 42–48.

[178] Andrey Mineev, Anatoli Bourmistrov, and Frode Mellemvik, eds., *Global Development in the Arctic: International Cooperation for the Future* (Routledge, 2023).

religion.[179] International conflict proceeds apace through legal-diplomatic wrangling over issues like control of space satellites and waste dispersal from an increasingly polluted planet. From its Cold War origins in the "Space Race" against the Soviet Union, the USA's space exploration under the National Aeronautics and Space Administration (NASA) continues. Now, however, the governmental framework includes the militarization of space, with one key development being the creation of a United States Space Force (USSF), founded in 2019.[180] The global superpower contest has developed an extra-terrestrial component. Extra-terrestrial exploration renews questions of what human life is, especially compared with other forms of life.

Toward common human betterment or destruction, exploration and development now proceed toward a radical rethinking of the human condition and the ideology of what it means to be human. Human rights debates often focus on the question of defining and conceptualizing rights. Today, however, humanity is increasingly confronted with the question of not only "what is a right?" but also "what is a human?" The transformative nature of Artificial Intelligence leads to hopeful and despairing possibilities for human development in a complex present and future.

Conclusion

Twentieth-century ideological warfare unleashed a global social reordering that continues. With humanitarianism as a remedy for violence, the chaos and reconstruction did not end with the disappearance of the Soviet Union in 1991. Consumerism has helped to reframe the global ideological struggle between Communism and Capitalism, with the Social Question no mere artifact of the nineteenth century. In the contemporary world, China is no longer a mission field for Europeans and Americans; it is now a vital global hegemon, including interactions that are reshaping Europe and America.

Also consider the position of Ireland in humanitarian politics in modern history: moving from being an object of despairing pity to becoming actively involved in humanitarian relief efforts and a beacon of future hope. In the nineteenth century, scores of people had emigrated from colonial Ireland to escape the devasting potato famine that killed around one million people, while the rest of the world observed an unfolding disaster in the British Empire. After a national independence movement in the twentieth century achieved state-hood via revolution and civil war, the Ireland that emerged from colonial

---

[179] Lily Kong and Orlando Woods, *Religion and Space: Competition, Conflict, and Violence in the Contemporary World* (Bloomsbury, 2016).

[180] For NASA, see www.nasa.gov/ last accessed December 8, 2023; for USSF, see www.space force.mil/ last accessed December 8, 2023.

subordination has undergone an amazing progressive transformation, becoming a neutral, independent state giving humanitarian aid to feed, stabilize, and rebuild post-1945 Europe.[181] The transnational Catholicism of Catholic Relief Services, and its Irish-American network operating between Ireland, America, and the Vatican, was a key part of these efforts. Mirroring their strong leadership roles in American and global Catholic society in the early twentieth century, Irish-American clerics formed most of CRS's leadership and had a historically informed sense of famine relief grounded in their transatlantic experiences. Alluding to the combination of governmental and NGO efforts, in a 1949 letter to CRS leadership, Cardinal Samuel Stritch of Chicago wrote, "The Irish Government has done a large work of relief and has been given little credit for it."[182] The legacies of transformative humanitarianism continue as Ireland, because of Brexit, finds itself positioned as the leading English-speaking country in the European Union, ranking near the top of the world's countries listed on the United Nations development indices for quality of life. Ireland is now a prosperous hub for global attention and foreign investment; nevertheless, it is a nation that on the streets of Dublin daily sees poignant scenes of homelessness and hunger for many people wanting a better life: for Irish citizens, as well as refugees, migrants, and asylum-seekers. Ireland has come a long way in a brief time in history, and there is much more social work to be done.

Modern historians do not like to view history primarily in terms of contemporary relevance, which can reflect the mores of the present and the subjectivity of the individual historian rather than the beliefs and actions of societies in the past. However, the problem of modern war and humanitarianism challenges this standpoint because it forces historians to confront their own subjectivities and limits of perspective while trying to understand the phenomena they are studying. This is especially difficult when discussing the place of ideology regarding questions of belief and unbelief.

Ideological humanitarianism in the modern world is situated at the nexus of humanitarianism and human rights, with religion being a vital part of the story. Analyzing religion in the contemporary age tends toward polemics of advocacy or condemnation, which has led to a neglect of critical nuanced histories of ideology. The history of religious humanitarianism during the First World War saw the emergence of humanitarian problems that required global frameworks, mobilizing resources to provide local solutions on a mass international scale.

---

[181] Jérôme aan de Wiel, *Ireland's Helping Hand to Europe: Combatting Hunger from Normandy to Tirana, 1945–1950* (New York, 2021).

[182] Catholic University of America Archives, NCWC, Series 1, subseries 1.1, Box 48, Folder 20: Letter, 14 September 1949, Cardinal Samuel Stritch to War Relief Services.

The slaughter of the wars, essential though it was to their outcomes, is nonetheless a misleading symbol of the effects of total war that did not end neatly in 1918 or 1945. The field of humanitarianism thus represents one of the wars' direct legacies that helped transform the modern world.

The secularization narrative of modernization theory dies hard. However, if one is serious about the relevance of religion in contemporary world politics, one must recognize that whatever degree of European secularization occurred during the nineteenth and twentieth centuries, sticking to the secularization framework seems increasingly antiquated, Eurocentric, and out of step with the awareness of the global relevance of religion. Instead of looking to Manichean narratives about the decline or triumph of either religion or secularism, one should examine the broad spectrum of belief and unbelief in complicated coexistence. Sacred and secular shifts have occurred globally and will continue to occur, and these trends resist easy categorization. In discussing narratives of dynamic change and the growth of humanitarian organizations, studies have shown that between World War II and the 1990s, private voluntary organizations increased dramatically, and the growth was in secular organizations. Since the 1990s, the resurgence has been in faith-based organizations.[183]

There are both quantitative and qualitative dimensions to the nature of religious humanitarianism. As Akira Iriye and others have shown, many studies of international organizations and global community-building marginalize religious organizations, especially with narrow definitions of NGOs that exclude religious organizations. In the aftermath of the Second World War, from 1946–1955, the largest volume of goods distributed abroad was by Catholic Relief Services; the Church World Service was third, and the Jewish Committee was fourth.[184] This neglect is remarkable because as the leading history of CRS points out, "In the post-war decades, over three-fourths of all voluntary aid from the American people to the needy overseas was donated by the three great faith-related agencies."[185]

The relationship of humanitarianism and human rights through the era of total war, 1914–1945, remains massively understudied. The post-1945 humanitarian organizations did not emerge like Athena from the head of Zeus. These organizations' founding principles, personnel, and actions were tested in the crucible

---

[183] Barnett and Stein, *Sacred Aid*, 5; Robert Barro and Rachel McLeary, "Private Voluntary Organizations Engaged in International Assistance, 1939– 2004," *Nonprofit and Voluntary Quarterly* 37, no. 3 (September 2008): 512–536. For an excellent overview of the data, see McLeary, *Global Compassion*.

[184] See Akira Iriye, *Global Community: The Role of International Organizations in the Making of the Global Community* (Berkeley, 2002), 50–51, citing Wallace J. Campbell, *The Story of CARE: A Personal Account* (New York, 1990), 110.

[185] Egan, *Catholic Relief Services*, 12.

of the First World War and its aftermath. Successes and failures helped to inform responses to the Second World War and its aftermath.

Faith-based humanitarian organizations in the post-1945 era can form crucial case studies for the transition from relief to development, thus enhancing histories of humanitarianism, human rights, and their relationships. As Michael Barnett has written, imagining humanitarianism and human rights can be thought of in terms of an ideal-type contrast: Humanitarianism aims to improve the world as it is, whereas the idea of human rights aims to improve the world as it should be. Humanitarianism and human rights have different frames of suffering. Humanitarianism mobilizes pity and sentiment for immediate action, trying to alleviate suffering in the present. Its watchwords are neutrality, impartiality, and independence. By contrast, the concept of human rights looks to a more long-term and legalistic future framework based on universalism and nondiscrimination, with states held accountable. Defining rights and rights violations, human rights thinking tends to think in legalistic terms, often invoking categories of victims and perpetrators, aiming for punishment, redress, and justice.[186]

Religiously informed humanitarianism also provokes scholars and the public to reexamine fundamental conditions of war and peace. The ideological dimension is inescapable for theorizing normative conditions of humane treatment and the conduct of war. Far from archaic ideas of angels dancing on the heads of pins, contemporary principles of humanitarianism help to inform notions of "just war" and the ideas of when wars end. Derived from the ancient schematics of Augustine and Aquinas, a new category of "just war," *ius post bellum* (justice after war), has been developed to theorize the normative conditions under which wars end. The question of how wars end informs not only the decision to go to war but also the questions of how human societies fight and help each other.[187] If this seems too abstract, consider the difficulty in naming an end date to the USA's wars and related conflicts in Afghanistan (begun 2001) and Iraq (begun 2003), as well as the continuing violence and rebuilding efforts in these societies.

The destructive and reconstructive legacies of wars do not have a convenient narrative fiction of a single date in history, even when most of the fighting seems to have stopped. Rethinking how wars end, and the suffering likely to occur, should inform decisions about whether to go to war at all. Questions of agency, involving action and inaction, are key: Who does what to whom, and who is responsible for fellow human beings? The decision not to help is also a form of action, both individually and collectively.

---

[186] Barnett, *Humanitarianism and Human Rights*, 8, 240.
[187] Brian Orend, *The Morality of War*, 2nd ed. (Broadview Press, 2006).

Most pointedly when dealing with the issue of genocide, it forces historians to confront complex, shifting categories of victims, resisters, bystanders, and perpetrators. Such questions have disturbing historical and contemporary implications. When reading about the genocides of the twentieth century, modern historians, and the public, like to believe that they would have resisted "evil" and "done the right thing." However, most responsible historical studies of genocide conclude that most people were, and are, bystanders and even perpetrators of violence in their own societies. Paralyzed by information overload, distance creates a sense of powerlessness when presented with constant news of people in trouble in faraway places. In the digital age of 24/7 news coverage when communication is instantaneous compared to the pre-1914 world, one must confront the reality of how people respond to news about war, violence, and other people in need. In times of global interconnection, "global citizens" must ask themselves how they should reach out to the most vulnerable and marginalized, both globally and locally. History judges both action and inaction.

When killing or helping each other, human beings acting in the public sphere are engaged in a contest of values about what kind of society they want. This is the case in times of war and peace. Thus, on a spectrum of belief and unbelief, the history of religious humanitarianism during the era of total war can inform how human societies on a fragile planet should work together toward peace, freedom, and prosperity for all.

Bibliography

Akçam, Taner, *The Young Turks' Crime against Humanity: The Armenian Genocide and Ethnic Cleansing in the Ottoman Empire* (Princeton: Princeton University Press, 2012).

Alterman, Jon ; and von Hippel, Karin, (eds.), *Understanding Islamic Charities* (Washington, DC: Center for Strategic & International Studies, 2007).

Barnett, Michael, *Empire of Humanity: A History of Humanitarianism* (Ithaca, NY: Cornell University Press, 2011).

Barnett, Michael (ed.), *Humanitarianism and Human Rights: A World of Differences?* (Cambridge: Cambridge University Press, 2020).

Barnett, Michael; and Stein, Janice Gross, (eds.), *Sacred Aid: Faith and Humanitarianism* (Oxford: Oxford University Press, 2012).

Barro, Robert; and McLeary, Rachel, "Private Voluntary Organizations Engaged in International Assistance, 1939–2004," *Nonprofit and Voluntary Quarterly* 37, no. 3 (September 2008): 512–536.

Bartov, Omer, *Mirrors of Destruction: War, Genocide, and Modern Identity* (Oxford: Oxford University Press, 2000).

Baughan, Emily, *Saving the Children: Humanitarianism, Internationalism, and Empire* (Berkeley, CA: University of California Press, 2021).

Bayly, C. A., *The Birth of the Modern World, 1780–1914* (Malden, MA: Wiley-Blackwell, 2004).

Bayly, C. A., *Remaking the Modern World 1900–2015: Global Connections and Comparisons* (Malden, MA: Wiley-Blackwell, 2018).

Betts, Paul, *Ruin and Renewal: Civilizing Europe after World War II* (New York: Basic Books, 2021).

Bloxham, Donald, *History and Morality* (Oxford: Oxford University Press, 2020).

Borgwardt, Elizabeth, *A New Deal for the World: America's Vision for Human Rights* (Cambridge, MA: The Belknap Press of Harvard University Press, 2005).

Borton, John; and Davey, Eleanor, "History and Practitioners: The Use of History by Humanitarians and Potential Benefits of History to the Humanitarian Sector," in Pedro Ramos Pinto and Bertrand Taithe, eds., *The Impact of History? Histories at the Beginning of the 21st Century* (London: Routledge, 2015), 153–168.

Cabanes, Bruno, *The Great War and the Origins of Humanitarianism, 1918–1924* (Cambridge: Cambridge University Press, 2014).

Calhoun, Craig; Juergensmeyer, Mark; and van Antwerpen, Jonathan (eds.), *Rethinking Secularism* (Oxford: Oxford University Press, 2011).

Clarke, Gerard; and Jennings, Michael, (eds.), *Development, Civil Society, and Faith-Based Organizations: Bridging the Sacred and the Secular* (New York: Palgrave, 2008).

Davis, Kenneth C., *More Deadly than War: The Hidden History of the Spanish Flu and the First World War* (New York: Henry Holt, 2018).

Egan, Eileen M., *Catholic Relief Services: The Beginning Years* (New York: Catholic Relief Services, 1988).

Fassin, Didier, *Humanitarian Reason: A Moral History of the Present Times*, trans. Rachel Gomme (Berkeley, CA: University of California Press, 2012).

Fehrenbach, Heide; and Rodogno, Davide, eds., *Humanitarian Photography: A History* (Cambridge: Cambridge University Press, 2015).

Ferris, Elizabeth, "Faith-Based and Secular Humanitarian Organizations," *International Review of the Red Cross* 87, no. 858 (2005): 311–325.

Figes, Orlando, *A People's Tragedy: The Russian Revolution, 1891–1924* (New York: Viking, 1997).

Forsythe, David P., *The Humanitarians: The International Committee of the Red Cross* (Cambridge: Cambridge University Press, 2005).

Foster, Elizabeth A., *African Catholic: Decolonization and the Transformation of the Church* (Cambridge, MA: Harvard University Press, 2019).

Furniss, Jamie; and Meier, Daniel, "La laïc et le religieux dans l'action humanitaire," *A Contrario: Revue Interdisciplinaire de Sciences Sociales* 18 (2012): 7–36.

Gatrell, Peter, *The Making of the Modern Refugee* (Oxford: Oxford University Press, 2013).

Gatrell, Peter, *The Unsettling of Europe: How Migration Reshaped a Continent* (New York: Basic Books, 2019).

Gatrell, Peter ; Gill, Rebecca ; Little, Branden ; and Piller, Elisabeth, "Discussion: Humanitarianism," in *1914–1918-online. International Encyclopedia of the First World War*, eds. Ute Daniel, Peter Gatrell, Oliver Janz, et al., eds., issued by Freie Universität Berlin, Berlin November 9, 2017. https://doi.org/10.15463/ie1418.11168; www.1914-1918-online.net.

Gerwarth, Robert; and Manela, Erez (eds.), *Empires at War, 1911–1923* (Oxford: Oxford University Press, 2014).

Geyer, Michael ; and Fitzpatrick, Sheila (eds.), *Beyond Totalitarianism: Stalinism and Nazism Compared* (Cambridge: Cambridge University Press, 2009).

Granick, Jaclyn, "Waging Relief: The Politics and Logistics of American Jewish War Relief in Europe and the Near East (1914–1918)," *First World War Studies* 5, no. 1 (2014): 55–68.

Granick, Jaclyn, *International Jewish Humanitarianism in the Age of the Great War* (Cambridge: Cambridge University Press, 2021).

Hirono, Miwa, "Three Legacies of Humanitarianism in China," *Disasters* 37, Supplement 2 (October 2013): S202–S220.

Horne, John; and Kramer, Alan, *German Atrocities 1914: A History of Denial* (New Haven, CT: Yale University Press, 2001).

Houlihan, Patrick J., *Catholicism and the Great War: Religion and Everyday Life in Germany and Austria-Hungary, 1914–1922* (Cambridge: Cambridge University Press, 2015).

Houlihan, Patrick J., "Renovating Christian Charity: Global Catholicism, the Save the Children Fund, and Humanitarianism during the First World War," *Past & Present* 250, no. 1 (February 2021): 203–241.

Ibhawoh, Bonny, *Human Rights in Africa* (Cambridge: Cambridge University Press, 2018).

Ickx, Johan, *Pio XII e gli ebrei. L'archivista del Vaticano rivela finalmente il ruolo di papa Pacelli durante la Seconda Guerra Mondiale*, trans. Rosa Prencipe, Caterina Chiappa, and Monica Pezzella (Milan: Mondadori Libri, 2021).

Irish, Tomás, *Feeding the Mind: Humanitarianism and the Reconstruction of European Intellectual Life, 1919–1933* (Cambridge: Cambridge University Press, 2023).

Iriye, Akira, *Global Community: The Role of International Organizations in the Making of the Global Community* (Berkeley, CA: University of California Press, 2002).

Irwin, Julia F., *Making the World Safe: The American Red Cross and a Nation's Humanitarian Awakening* (Oxford: Oxford University Press, 2013).

Jenkins, Philip, *The Next Christendom: The Coming of Global Christianity*, 3rd ed. (Oxford: Oxford University Press, 2011).

Jenkins, Philip, *The Great and Holy War: How World War I Became a Religious Crusade* (New York: HarperOne, 2014).

Johnson, Todd M. and Ross, Kenneth R. (eds.), *Atlas of Global Christianity* (Edinburgh: University of Edinburgh Press, 2009).

Johnson, Todd M. and Zurlo, Gina A. (eds.), *World Christian Database* (Leiden: Brill, 2023).

Jones, Heather, "International or Transnational? Humanitarian Action during the First World War," *European Review of History: Revue européenne d'histoire* 16, no. 5 (2009): 697–713.

Kertzer, David I., *The Pope at War: The Secret History of Pius XII, Mussolini, and Hitler* (New York: Random House, 2022).

King, David P., *God's Internationalists: World Vision and the Age of Evangelical Humanitarianism* (Philadelphia: University of Pennsylvania Press, 2015).

Kong, Lily ; and Woods, Orlando, *Religion and Space: Competition, Conflict, and Violence in the Contemporary World* (London: Bloomsbury, 2016).

Koschorke, Klaus; Ludwig, Frieder ; and Delgado, Mariano (eds.), *A History of Christianity in Asia, Africa, and Latin America, 1450–1990: A Documentary Sourcebook* (Grand Rapids, MI: William B. Eerdmans, 2007).

Dal Lago, Enrico; and O'Sullivan, Kevin, "Introduction: Towards a New History of Humanitarianism. Moving the Social," *Journal of Social History and the History of Social Movements* 57 (2017): 5–20.

Lempereur, Alain, "Humanitarian Negotiation to Protect: John Rabe and the Nanking International Safety Zone (1937–1938)," *Group Decision & Negotiation* 25, no. 4 (July 2016): 663–691.

Li, Yannan, "Red Cross Society in Imperial China, 1904–1912: A Historical Analysis," *Voluntas* 27 (2016): 2274–2291.

Little, Branden, "An Explosion of New Endeavours: Global Humanitarian Responses to Industrialized Warfare in the First World War Era," *First World War Studies* 5 (2014): 1–16.

Liulevicius, Vejas Gabriel, *War Land on the Eastern Front: Culture, National Identity and German Occupation in World War I* (Cambridge: Cambridge University Press, 2000).

Lobo, Bryan ; Morali, Ilaria; and Pinto, Rolphy (eds.), *Maximum Illud: La Missione Tra Storia e Attualità* (Rome: Gregorian & Biblical Press, 2020).

MacCulloch, Diarmaid, *A History of Christianity: The First Three Thousand Years* (New York: Viking, 2009).

Manela, Erez, *The Wilsonian Moment: Self Determination and the International Origins of Anticolonial Nationalism* (Oxford: Oxford University Press, 2007).

Mark James et al., *Socialism Goes Global: The Soviet Union and Eastern Europe in the Age of Decolonisation* (Oxford: Oxford University Press, 2022).

Maul, Daniel, "The Politics of Neutrality – Quaker Relief and the Spanish Civil War 1936–1939," *European Review of History: Revue européenne d'histoire* 23, no. 1–2 (2016): 82–100.

Mawdsley, Evan, *World War II: A New History,* 2nd ed. (Cambridge: Cambridge University Press, 2020).

McCleary, Rachel M., *Global Compassion: Private Voluntary Organizations and U.S. Foreign Policy since 1939* (Oxford: Oxford University Press, 2009).

McGreevy, John T., *Catholicism: A Global History from the French Revolution to Pope Francis* (New York: WW Norton, 2022).

Mendes-Flohr, Paul, *Martin Buber: A Life of Faith and Dissent* (New Haven, CT: Yale University Press, 2019).

Mineev, Andrey ; Bourmistrov, Anatoli; and Mellemvik, Frode (eds.), *Global Development in the Arctic: International Cooperation for the Future* (Abingdon: Routledge, 2023).

Mitter, Rana ; and Johnson, Elsbeth, "What the West Gets Wrong about China," *Harvard Business Review* 99, no. 3 (2021): 42–48.

Möller, Esther; Paulmann, Johannes; and Katharina Stornig (eds.), *Gendering Global Humanitarianism in the Twentieth Century: Practice, Politics and the Power of Representation* (New York: Palgrave, 2020).

Moses, A. Dirk, *Empire, Colony, Genocide: Conquest, Occupation and Subaltern Resistance in World History* (New York: Berghahn Books, 2008).

Nash, George H., *The Life of Herbert Hoover: The Humanitarian, 1914–1917* (New York: WW Norton, 1988).

Neubauer, Jack, "Adopting Revolution: The Chinese Communist Revolution and the Politics of Global Humanitarianism," *Modern China* 47, no. 5 (2021): 598–627.

Orend, Brian, *The Morality of War*, 2nd ed. (Petersborough: Broadview Press, 2006).

Osterhammel, Jürgen, *The Transformation of the World: A Global History of the Nineteenth Century*, trans. Patrick Camiller (Princeton, NJ: Princeton University Press, 2014).

Overy, Richard, *Blood and Ruins: The Last Imperial War, 1931–1945* (New York: Penguin, 2022).

Paulmann, Johannes, "Conjunctures in the History of International Humanitarian Aid during the Twentieth Century," *Humanity: An International Journal of Human Rights, Humanitarianism, and Development* 4, no. 2 (2013): 215–238.

Paulmann, Johannes, (ed.), *Dilemmas of Humanitarian Aid in the Twentieth Century* (Oxford: Oxford University Press, 2016).

Pedersen, Susan, *The Guardians: The League of Nations and the Crisis of Empire* (Oxford: Oxford University Press, 2015).

Pendas, Devin O., "Toward a New Politics? On the Recent Historiography of Human Rights," *Contemporary European History* 21, no. 1 (2012): 95–111.

Phillips, Howard, "'17, '18, '19: Religion and Science in Three Pandemics, 1817, 1918, and 2019," *Journal of Global History* 15, no. 3 (2020): 434–443.

Phillips, Howard ; and Killingray, David, (eds.), *The Spanish Influenza Pandemic of 1918–1919* (New York: Routledge, 2003).

Piller, Elisabeth, "German Child Distress, American Humanitarian Aid and Revisionist Politics, 1918–1924," *Journal of Contemporary History* 51, no. 3 (July 2016): 453–486.

Piller, Elisabeth, "American War Relief, Cultural Mobilization and the Myth of Impartial Humanitarianism, 1914–17," *Journal of the Gilded Age and Progressive Era* 17, no. 4 (October 2018): 619–635.

Pollard, John F., *The Papacy in the Age of Totalitarianism, 1914–1958* (Oxford: Oxford University Press, 2014).

Porter, Stephen, "Humanitarian Politics and Governance: International Responses to the Civilian Toll in the Second World War," in Michael Geyer and Adam Tooze, eds., *Cambridge History of the Second World War*, 3 vols. (Cambridge: Cambridge University Press, 2015), 3: 502–527.

Preston, Andrew, *Sword of the Spirit, Shield of Faith: Religion in American War and Diplomacy* (New York: Knopf, 2012).

Proctor, Tammy M., *Civilians in a World at War, 1914–1918* (New York: New York University Press, 2010).

Reinisch, Jessica, "Relief in the Aftermath of War," *Journal of Contemporary History* 43, no. 3 (2008): 371–404.

Reinisch, Jessica, "'We Shall Rebuild Anew a Powerful Nation': UNRRA, Internationalism and National Reconstruction in Poland," *Journal of Contemporary History* 43, no. 3 (2008): 451–476.

Reinisch, Jessica, "Internationalism in Relief: The Birth (and Death) of UNRRA," *Past & Present* 210, no. 6 (2011): 258–289.

Reinisch, Jessica, "Auntie UNRRA at the Crossroads," *Past & Present* 218, no. 8 (2013): 70–97.

Rodogno, Davide, *Against Massacre: Humanitarian Interventions in the Ottoman Empire, 1815–1914* (Princeton, NJ: Princeton University Press, 2011).

Rodogno, Davide, *Night on Earth: A History of International Humanitarianism in the Near East, 1918–1930* (Cambridge: Cambridge University Press, 2021).

Salih, M. A. Mohamed, "Islamic NGOs in Africa: The Promise and Peril of Islamic Voluntarism," in Alex de Waal, ed., *Islamism and Its Enemies in the Horn of Africa* (Bloomington: Indiana University Press, 2004), 146–181.

Salvatici, Silvia, *A History of Humanitarianism, 1789-Present: In the Name of Others*, trans. Philip Sanders (Manchester: Manchester University Press, 2015).

Scheer, Monique, *Rosenkranz und Kriegsvisionen: Marienerscheinungskulte im 20. Jahrhundert* (Tübingen: Tübinger Vereinigung für Volkskunde, 2006).

Shephard, Ben, "'Becoming Planning Minded': The Theory and Practice of Relief, 1940–1945," *Journal of Contemporary History* 43, no. 3 (2008): 405–419.

Shine, Cormac, "Papal Diplomacy by Proxy? Catholic Internationalism at the League of Nations' International Committee on Intellectual Cooperation, 1922–1939," *Journal of Ecclesiastical History* 69, no.4 (2018): 785–805.

Slezkine, Yuri, *The House of Government: A Saga of the Russian Revolution* (Princeton, NJ: Princeton University Press, 2017).

Smolkin, Victoria, *A Sacred Space Is Never Empty: A History of Soviet Atheism* (Princeton, NJ: Princeton University Press, 2018).

Spadaro, Antonio (ed.), *Anticipare il futuro della Cina. Ritratto di Mons. Aloysius Jin Luxian S.I.* (Vatican City: Incroci, 2020).

Stahl, Ronit Y., *Enlisting Faith: How the Military Chaplaincy Shaped Religion and State in Modern America* (Cambridge, MA: Harvard University Press, 2017).

Stanley, Brian, *Christianity in the Twentieth Century: A World History* (Princeton, NJ: Princeton University Press, 2018).

O'Sullivan, Kevin ; Hilton, Matthew ; and Fiori, Juliano, "Humanitarianisms in Context: Histories of Non-state Actors, from the Local to the Global," Special Issue, *European Review of History: Revue Européenne d'Histoire* 23, no. 1–2 (2016): 1–15.

O'Sullivan, Kevin, *The NGO Moment: The Globalisation of Compassion from Biafra to Live Aid* (Cambridge: Cambridge University Press, 2021).

Suny, Ronald Grigor, *"They Can Live in the Desert but Nowhere Else": A History of the Armenian Genocide* (Princeton, NJ: Princeton University Press, 2015).

Taithe, Bertrand, "The 'Making' of the Origins of Humanitarianism," *Contemporanea* 18, no. 3 (2015): 485–492.

Tanielian, Melanie S., *The Charity of War: Famine, Humanitarian Aid, and World War I in the Middle East* (Palo Alto, CA: Stanford University Press, 2018).

Taylor, Charles, *A Secular Age* (Cambridge, MA: The Belknap Press of Harvard University Press, 2007).

Tusan, Michelle, "Genocide, Famine and Refugees on Film: Humanitarianism and the First World War," *Past & Present* 237, no. 1 (November 2017): 197–235.

de Waal, Alex (ed.), *Islamism and Its Enemies in the Horn of Africa* (London: Hurst, 2004).

de Waal, Alex, "The Humanitarians' Tragedy: Escapable and Inescapable Cruelties," *Disasters* S2 (2010): S130–S137.

Watenpaugh, Keith David, *Bread from Stones: The Middle East and the Making of Modern Humanitarianism* (Berkeley, CA, : University of California Press, 2015).

Weitz, Eric D., *A World Divided: The Global Struggle for Human Rights in the Age of Nation-States* (Princeton, NJ: Princeton University Press, 2019).

aan de Wiel, Jérôme, *Ireland's Helping Hand to Europe: Combatting Hunger from Normandy to Tirana, 1945–1950* (New York: Central European University Press, 2021).

Wieters, Heike, *The NGO CARE and Food Aid from America, 1945–80: "Showered with Kindness"?* (Manchester: Manchester University Press, 2020).

Wilcox, Vanda (ed.), *Italy in the Era of the Great War* (Leiden: Brill, 2018).

Winter, Jay, "The Second Great War," *Revista Universitaria de Historia Militar* 7, no.14 (2018): 160–179.

Winter, Jay, *The Cultural History of War in the Twentieth Century and After* (Cambridge: Cambridge University Press, 2022).

Winter, Jay ; and Prost, Antoine, *The Great War in History and Historiography* (Cambridge: Cambridge University Press, 2011).

Woodbridge, George, *UNRRA: The History of the United Nations Relief and Rehabilitation Administration*, 3 vols. (New York: Columbia University Press, 1950).

Wu, Albert Monshan, *From Christ to Confucius: German Missionaries, Chinese Christians, and the Globalization of Christianity, 1860–1950* (New Haven, CT: Yale University Press, 2018).

Wylie, Neville ; Oppenheimer, Melanie; and Crossland, James (eds.), *The Red Cross Movement: Myths, Practices and Turning Points* (Manchester: Manchester University Press, 2020).

Cambridge Elements ≡

Modern Wars

General Editor

Robert Gerwarth
University College Dublin

Robert Gerwarth is Professor of Modern History at University College Dublin and Director of UCD's Centre for War Studies. He has published widely on the history of political violence in twentieth-century Europe, including an award-winning history of the aftermath of the Great War, *The Vanquished*, and a critically acclaimed biography of Reinhard Heydrich, the chief organizer of the Holocaust. He is also the general editor of Oxford University Press's *Greater War* series, and, with Jay Winter, general editor of Cambridge University Press's *Studies in the Social and Cultural History of Modern* Warfare series.

Editorial Board

Heather Jones, *University College London*
Rana Mitter, *University of Oxford*
Michelle Moyd, *Michigan State University*
Martin Thomas, *University of Exeter*

About the Series

Focusing on the flourishing field of war studies (broadly defined to include social, cultural and political perspectives), Elements in Modern Wars examine the forms, manifestations, and legacies of violence in global contexts from the mid-nineteenth century to the present day.

Cambridge Elements ≡

Modern Wars

Elements in the Series

The Cultural History of War in the Twentieth Century and After
Jay Winter

Warrior Women: The Cultural Politics of Armed Women, c.1850–1945
Alison S. Fell

Religious Humanitarianism during the World Wars, 1914–1945: Between Atheism and Messianism
Patrick J. Houlihan

A full series listing is available at: www.cambridge.org/EMOW